List of Tables

List of Tables

NOTE:
1. When works *in Japanese* are cited, the names of the authors are given in the Japanese style—surname first, personal name second; elsewhere, the English style is followed.
2. The value of the yen may be taken as ¥ 1,000 = £1

INDUSTRIAL DUALISM
IN JAPAN

INDUSTRIAL DUALISM IN JAPAN

A PROBLEM OF
ECONOMIC GROWTH AND STRUCTURAL CHANGE

A.

SEYMOUR BROADBRIDGE

111

ALDINE PUBLISHING COMPANY

Chicago

First published 1966 by
ALDINE PUBLISHING COMPANY
320 West Adams Street,
Chicago, Illinois 60606

FRANK CASS & CO. LTD.

Library of Congress Catalog Card Number 66-23159

Printed in Great Britain

Contents

Acknowledgements

My thanks are due to the School of Oriental and African Studies, University of London, for granting me leave in the session of 1963–64 to study in Japan, and to the Association for Asian Studies for financing a visit to the United States in 1963 to attend a conference on the Economic Modernization of Japan. I am also indebted to the Director of the Institute of Social Science, Tokyo University, who appointed me a Visiting Scholar of the Institute and who, together with his staff, gave me so much hospitality, help, and encouragement during the very pleasant months of my visit. Also, my family would wish to join me in acknowledging the great kindness of Professor Kōhachirō Takahashi, Professor and Mrs Kiyoshi Ōshima, Mr and Mrs Y. Fukushima, and Mr Kiyoshi Yamamoto.

In the years since 1959, when I first began to study the Japanese language and Japanese economic development, I have greatly benefited from contact with many specialists in England and the United States, but I should like to express a special debt to Professor F. J. Daniels and Dr P. G. O'Neill, of the School of Oriental and African Studies, and to Professor W. W. Lockwood, of Princeton University. Professor G. C. Allen was kind enough to criticise the first draft of this work but I alone am responsible for its inadequacies.

S. A. BROADBRIDGE

B

Preface

JAPAN is now one of the leading industrial nations of the world, yet its economy and its industry are still described as 'dualistic'. Huge combines co-exist with thousands of small businesses, and there are wide gaps in productivity and wages, gaps which are not present to anything like the same extent in the most advanced economies of the West. This essay explores some of the contrasts in Japanese industrial structure. First of all, the persistence of economic dualism during the years of extremely rapid economic growth since the Second World War is noted in the Introduction to Part I. This is followed by a survey of the origins of industrial dualism in Japan. These origins can be found in the effects of forced industrialisation as a follower nation under pressure from the West, and of the policies of the highly centralised and powerful governments of post-Restoration Japan. Chapter 2 gives an outline of economic growth and structure since the Second World War, and highlights those features which appear to have ensured the continuation of Japan's dual industrial structure. In Part II, Chapter 3 presents statistics of industrial scale and of wage and productivity differentials, and briefly surveys the dilemma which any government that is set on both economic modernisation and social and political stability must face in a dualistic economy. Some illustrations of the relationships, which are so important in Japanese dualism, between large and small firms and between small and even smaller firms, are provided in Chapter 4, and, finally, a Conclusion considers current economic policy and its effects on small businesses, and takes a look at future possibilities.

There is vast literature on economic and industrial dualism in Japan, but much of it is not readily available to the English student. Professor Allen's contribution on industrial growth and structure to E. B. Schumpeter *et al, The Industrialization of Japan and Manchukuo 1930–1940*, New York, 1940, is still one of the most valuable surveys in the English language, although it has, unfortunately, long been out of print. Miyohei Shinohara's important *Survey of Japanese Literature on the Small Industry*, Hitotsubashi University, Tokyo, 1964, is as yet available only as a privately circulated publication. This essay is intended to be a modest supplement to these works.

S. A. BROADBRIDGE
London, May 1965

PART I

THE ORIGINS AND DEVELOPMENT OF
INDUSTRIAL DUALISM IN JAPAN

INTRODUCTION

Post-War Economic Growth
and the
Persistence of Economic Dualism

I

In a characteristically gloomy comment on a huge 24% increase in industrial production in 1953 the *Economic Survey of Japan (1953–1954)* dismissed the spectacular leaps in the indices as 'sham prosperity in contrast to West Germany's economic recovery which the world calls miraculous'.[1] Ten years later, after an unprecedented run of high growth rates, official economists were still dissatisfied:[2]

> . . . as far as the economic scale is concerned, the Japanese economy, as a result of its high growth during the past 18 years, has managed to reach the level of the economic scales of advanced countries in the world.
>
> However, during the process of high economic growth, imbalances were created in various sectors of the economy and it is pointed out that there were some aspects which were unbecoming to an advanced industrial nation.

In the eyes of many, one of these 'unbecoming' aspects is undoubtedly economic dualism, a problem which has attracted more, not less, attention as Japan has climbed into the front rank of industrial powers.

Table 1 shows how rapid Japan's economic advance has been in the years since the end of the Korean War: between 1953 and 1962 real gross national product increased by an average of over 9% per annum. If the whole post-war period is taken the growth rate averages 10%, but there is a strong case for ignoring the years between 1947 and 1953 since they may reasonably be regarded as the 'recovery years'. The growth rate was even higher in that period: an average of 11% between 1947 and 1953, and 12% during the three years of

3

Industrial Dualism in Japan

TABLE 1: *Annual Growth Rates of Real Gross National Product in Japan, 1953–1962* (%)

Fiscal Year	Annual Growth Rate	Fiscal Year	Annual Growth Rate
1953–54	6·7	1958–59	3·2
1954–55	3·3	1959–60	17·9
1955–56	10·3	1960–61	13·3
1956–57	9·0	1961–62	14·0
1957–58	7·9	1962–63	5·9

Sources: Ōkita Saburo, *Nihon keizai no seichō to kōzō* (The Growth and Structure of the Japanese Economy), Tokyo, 1962, p. 64.
Keizai Kikaku-chō (Economic Planning Agency), *Kokumin shotoku hakusho Shōwa 37 nendo* (National Income White Paper for 1962–63), Tokyo, 1964, p. 163.

the Korean War. But real expenditure on personal consumption did not reach the level of 1934–36 (usually taken as the pre-war norm) until 1953–54,[4] so any attempt to discuss the various factors contributing to Japan's impressive post-war record must take into account the margin that existed between 1947 and 1953 for mere recovery. Even so, the average growth rate of 9% marked up after 1953 was a considerable achievement. This is a high, though not exceptionally high, average compared with other periods of rapid expansion. Between 1905 and 1912 growth averaged 6·7%, between 1912 and 1919 the figure was 7%, and the 1930's recorded an even higher rate of 7·5%. As Professors Ohkawa and Rosovsky have pointed out, an interesting and important characteristic of growth since 1953, compared with these other periods of fast development, is the absence of negative or even very low positive rates of growth. This, rather than unusually high rates is, they believe, the thing that distinguishes the post-war period.[5]. It can be seen from Table 1 that growth was sustained at a high level until 1959, and then jumped still higher during the boom of 1959–1961 when it averaged just over 15%. Yet another very high rate was achieved in 1963–64 against all expectations: the forecast of 8·2% made towards the end of the fiscal year was much too low, and national product increased by 12·3%. This time, at least, there might be agreement that growth had now become exceptional: over a period of five years the rate of expansion had moved up to an average of 12·7%, and the only other period of Japanese economic history that can remotely compare with this record were the years of the First World War.

In 1964 Japan had developed so fast from the poverty-stricken levels of 1945 that she had supplanted Britain as the fourth largest industrial power and may even have exceeded West Germany's total industrial production. Certainly she leads the world in shipbuilding—four million tons in 1964, which was four times the output of Britain's shipbuilding industry—motor-cycles, transistor radios and other items such as pianos. She comes second only to the United States in commercial vehicles, television, synthetic fibres, textiles and heavy electric machines, while in steel and cement she now ranks above all others barring the United States and Soviet Russia.

It is important to note that explanations of Japan's rapid growth now put less stress on temporary factors and more on longer-term pressures towards a high growth rate. No one denies the influence of the recovery factor, of the Korean War and American aid and off-shore procurement, and of other special causes such as the demographic change which has resulted in an exceptionally high working population ratio. But economic development has, over a long period since about 1880, been more rapid in Japan than in other advanced countries, and some economists have found the concept of 'dualism' an illuminating tool in their attempts to isolate the important causes of this fast growth. It is true that the strong Marxist leanings of many Japanese economists leads to a persistent use of terminology which one does not find in the work of most western economists and which gives pungency and anger to many analyses of Japan's dual economy and dual industrial structure. These analyses are further characterised by great pessimism about Japan's future development. It is therefore all the more interesting that one of Japan's leading economists, who does not share these attitudes, should rate 'capital concentration and the dual economy' to be one of 'the most important ingredients' in Japan's high rate of growth.[6]

II

Today [the] economy is a mixture of two phases of economic development. On the one side, it contains a highly developed sector, which is characterised by the hired-labour system, large-scale operations, and modern, capital-using methods of production, and which yields to those working in it a reasonably high income per head. On the other side, it contains a large 'pre-industrial' or 'pre-capitalistic' sector, which is based predominantly on artisan or family labour, minutely small-scale operations and a minimum provision of capital, and which provides for those working in it only a very low income per head. This mixture sets [the] economy apart from the 'advanced' economies where small-scale enterprise has survived only to a much more limited extent and where no such marked cleavage in income levels exists. . . .

After some eighty years of industrial development along modern lines, the . . . economy has remained roughly a half-and-half system. This system . . . I shall call . . . the 'dual economy'. . . .

'Economic dualism' . . . exists within both agriculture and industry, as well as between agriculture and industry, even if the greater part of the poor group is to be found in agriculture.

This quotation comes, not from any work on Japan, but from Vera Lutz's book on Italian economic development.[7] Yet in its essentials it is remarkably appropriate to the Japanese economy and it seems, therefore, that even when we have narrowed down the world to the big industrial powers Japan's problems of dualism are not unique. This is not likely to be of much consolation to the many Japanese who tend to write as though they are, and who in any case usually compare their economy with the economies of north-western Europe and North America. Furthermore, no book written on industrial dualism in Japan could say as little as Dr Lutz says about sub-contracting—a practice which in Japan at least is often regarded as one of the most prominent distinguishing characteristics of Japanese industry.

So while we may acknowledge the existence of economic dualism in other countries and more particularly in those, like Spain and Italy, which have in the last decade or so also experienced fairly rapid economic growth and improvements in living standards, we must still recognise the force of Japanese criticism of Japanese backwardness, of 'pre-capitalist' or 'feudalistic' economic relationships, and 'parasitic' exploitation of small-scale businesses. Japan is now, after all, a much stronger industrial power than these other countries, is therefore a more vital part of the international economic community,[8] and should therefore, it is argued, be as 'modern' as the most modern. Japanese critics would certainly agree with the mood of Dr Lutz's concluding remarks that a high growth rate, increased employment in manufacturing, absorption of unemployed and sectoral transfer of labour may yet leave largely unsolved 'the problem of *under-employment*-the essence of the economic dualism' with which she was concerned.[9] When the current ten-year economic plan to double Japanese national income was published, government economists expressed the view that the problem of dual structure[10]

> ... is deeply rooted in the economy and society of this country and, therefore, it is not of such a nature as will be solved naturally when the economy develops at a high rate.

Implicit here is a comment on the belief that as an economy progresses toward the scale of the most advanced western economies so will the excessive number of excessively small industrial units decrease; that the structure of the economy—the balance between agriculture and industry—will change, bringing not only a steady diminution of agriculture's share in the national product but an equivalent reduction in the proportion of gainfully employed working on the land. In other words, that growth, by itself, necessarily causes a more rational distribution of all factors, including labour. Evidently this always happens to some extent but the crux of the problem in Japan is precisely the combination of, on the one hand, a growing and prosperous industry with a poor agriculture, which nevertheless absorbs a much higher proportion of the working population than in other advanced industrial countries, and on the other hand, the resilience of the small-scale sector in industry itself. As we shall see, the small enterprise sector accounts for a very high proportion of employment, and contributes a substantial proportion of total output, but wage and productivity differentials are great.

REFERENCES

1 Economic Counsel Board, Japanese Government, Tokyo, 1954, p. 1.

2 Economic Planning Agency, Japanese Government, *Economic Survey of Japan (1962–1963)*, Tokyo, n.d. [1963], p. 1.

3 Cf. *National Income White Paper for 1962–63, loc. cit.* All years referred to are fiscal years. Thus 1952–53 is taken as the last year of the Korean War.

4 *Ibid.*, p. 165.

5 Kazushi Ohkawa and Henry Rosovsky, 'Recent Japanese Growth in Historical Perspective', *American Economic Review*, Vol. LIII, No. 2, May, 1963, pp. 578–579.

6 Miyohei Shinohara, *Growth and Cycles in the Japanese Economy*, Tokyo, 1962, p. 25.

7 Vera Lutz, *Italy: a Study in Economic Development*, London, 1962, pp. 3 and 4.

8 In 1964 Japan transferred to 8th Article status in the International Monetary Fund, and was granted full membership of O.E.C.D.

9 V. Lutz, *op. cit.*, pp. 328–329.

10 Economic Planning Agency, Japanese Government, *New Long-Range Economic Plan of Japan (1961–1970)*, Tokyo, 1961, p. 10.

CHAPTER 1

The Origins

of

Industrial Dualism

I

Modern industrial development could not take place in Japan while the policy of seclusion enforced by the Tokugawa family, who were the effective rulers of Japan from the early 1600s to 1868, continued to insulate both the economy and social structure from the impact of the major international powers. In order to redress the distortion caused by over-emphasis on the catastrophic and catalytic effect of the arrival of arrogant westerners demanding trade and diplomatic relations, historians have exposed the internal strains and developments which were destroying the feudal structure so carefully established and brilliantly maintained by the Tokugawa *Shōgun*, or military dictators, for over 200 years. The economic decline of the *samurai* class, the dissatisfaction of the commercial classes with their social and political status—a dissatisfaction which found intellectual expression—and the agricultural and industrial changes taking place in rural Japan were producing a widespread desire for political change. But the decision of the western powers that Japan must be forced to open its doors was just as important a determinant of the pattern of her subsequent development as it was of China's from the 1840s. Marius Jansen has insisted 'that the outstanding intellectual and political experience in the formative years of the Restoration activists was the discovery that their society was incapable of successful resistance to the Western threat'.[1]

The changes that had occurred before the arrival in 1853 of Commodore Perry, with his American warships and his demands for formal relations with Japan, were crucial to the extent that they had produced a society which, although it was impotent with its existing administration, *was* capable of transforming itself swiftly enough and successfully enough to avoid the disaster that engulfed China. The political groups that coalesced during the last fifteen years of the Tokugawa regime, and in the end overthrew the last *Shōgun* and restored the Emperor Meiji to his rightful place, had widely differing social and political aims, but those who were to lead Japan in the first decades of its 'modern' century assumed, perhaps correctly, that the only way to withstand the pressure of the West was to adopt as many western ideas and techniques as seemed essential to the creation of a society and an economy which would be, at one and the same time, acceptable in the international community, yet formidable obstacles to western aggression.

It was also assumed that time was limited: Japan modernised during the decades of western expansion in India, China, and the Pacific generally, and in Africa, to list only the more relevant of the areas affected by western imperialism, and the sense of urgency was yet another important influence that was exerted on the pattern of economic growth as a result of Japan's injection into the international economy. This urgency necessitated economic policies which, it will be argued, made almost inevitable the creation of a dual industrial structure, while the pattern of social and economic behaviour that was built up in a country isolated from all but minor contacts with the outside world for more than two centuries, not only facilitated these policies, but also played an important independent part in bringing about industrial dualism.

II

Economic growth and industrial structure result from the inter-action of a complex variety of factors and in a sense, therefore, every-thing that happens in a society is relevant. In this essay the principal objects of enquiry are industrial structure and industrial dualism, but there will be no need to labour the obvious point that the wider dualism—the disparity between industrial and agricultural sectors—is also relevant. Furthermore, once one turns to the historical origins of dualism and to the relationship between dualism and the process of economic growth, the necessity of considering the labour market and capital supplies automatically draws in agriculture. Then there are government policy, the influence of the West, and other factors to take into account. But if all things are relevant, some are certainly more relevant than others, and it is believed that among the deter-minants of industrial structure in modern Japan the following five elements were particularly important in the development of industrial dualism:

1. Government policies and the rise of the *zaibatsu*.
2. The structure of the capital and money markets.
3. The dependence on imported technology and techniques.
4. The consumption and saving habits of the Japanese; and
5. The structure of the labour market and the pattern of agricultural development.

1. Government Policies and the Rise of the *Zaibatsu*

As in Prussia and then Imperial Germany in the same period, great efforts were made to improve the military and economic strength of Japan in response to international political and economic trends. Both countries imposed strong central direction, built up powerful military forces and engaged in wars, stimulated heavy industry, and favoured the growth of powerful industrial combines. In Japan the clarion call of the Meiji period was *fukoku-kyōhei*: 'a rich country, a strong army'.[2] Opinions might differ on where emphasis should be laid—whether or not Japan should make an early attempt to assert herself militarily was one point of controversy—but there was consensus on the desirability of developing modern industries, and of lessening economic dependence on western countries. For some decades after 1868 Japan was without an ocean-going mercantile marine and her external trade was almost completely in the hands of foreigners. She possessed no shipbuilding industry capable of supporting an independent shipping industry, and, going further down the economic scale, no iron and steel industry to supply yards, and no machine industry to fit out plants. The government stepped in to help development in all these sectors, and although the early efforts were followed by a withdrawal in the 1880s, in the 1890s and at the turn of the century several important measures were adopted by the government: the special banks were created: the Gold Standard was adopted with the help of the large indemnity from China after Japan's victory in the Sino-Japanese War; laws were passed to stimulate the shipping and shipbuilding industries; and it was decided to establish the state-owned Yawata Iron Works. By 1914 Japan, though still far from her goal of economic independence in strategic industries, had made substantial progress. In 1913 domestic production of merchant ships equalled imports.[3] In 1914 the Yawata Works was still only capable of supplying rather less than a quarter of the shipbuilding industry's steel requirements, but in 1900 Japan had had to import 99% of her total steel consumption.[4]

The impact of government policies on output and investment patterns was tremendous. Writing on the period 1887–1940 Professor Rosovsky has said:[5]

> Throughout the entire fifty-three years, government was the largest and most important investor in the economy. Its share of domestic capital formation never averaged less than 40%, and it was only very rarely that low.

In addition, government sales of plant, government contracts and government subsidies all helped to concentrate the development of transportation and heavy industry in the hands of a small group of families—the *zaibatsu*. Professor Tsuchiya has pointed out that while it would be an exaggeration to identify the history of 'political merchants'—businessmen who had close financial and political links with factions in government and bureaucracy—with the history of the *zaibatsu*, there is no doubt that they run parallel: the success of the political merchants and the formation of Japanese capitalism were inextricably linked. Most of the *zaibatsu* were founded by those political merchants who had very close connections with the *hanbatsu* (clansmen) of the early Meiji government, and who made good use of the government contracts awarded to them and of the government enterprises which were sold off in the 1880s.[6] These *zaibatsu* received powerful stimuli from the government military and naval programmes, and, more particularly, from the Sino-Japanese War of 1894–95.[7] The development of heavy industries and marine transportation did not really get under way until the period 1890–1910, which spanned both the Sino- and the Russo-Japanese Wars. It was in these years that combines like Mitsubishi, founded primarily on Yatarō Iwasaki's successful cornering of military transportation contracts, and destined to be one of the world's greatest shipbuilding, engineering, commercial and financial combines, rose to a powerful position in the Japanese economy.[8]

It is not suggested that these groups, or others like them, would have enjoyed no expansion without government connections and government policies of support. The sale of state-owned businesses in the early 1880s to private interests was probably due more to the government's financial difficulties than to any concrete plan of strengthening a small clique of businessmen who supported new policies of expansion.[9] But it would not have been so fast, nor so extensive, and it is, in any case, difficult to separate government stimulus from 'natural' economic development in Japan.[10] There can be little argument over the vital role of the state in many branches of industrial activity both between 1868 and 1881,[11] and in later decades, and in quantitative terms, Rosovsky's analysis of government investment and military demands is a very convincing proof of the pervading influence of the state on the pattern of economic growth and change.

In the decades between 1910 and 1940 the *zaibatsu* increased their strength, gathering more and more of the nation's industrial and financial resources into their networks, and it was precisely in this period that substantial wage differentials in manufacturing industry appeared. In 1909 workers in plants of fewer than 1000 employees received wages which were over 90% of the wages obtained in large-scale plants employing over 1000. By 1925 the differentials had widened considerably, with, for example, workers in plants with payrolls of from 100 to 500 receiving only 84% of the wages paid in the biggest plants. These differentials continued to grow until the outbreak of the Second World War.[12] The *zaibatsu* and some other large concerns, producing the goods and services of western industrialization, were one side of the dual industrial structure. The contrasting side of industrial dualism—the tiny, small, and medium-sized enterprises—also grew, expanding into millions of units in industry and commerce. Many were complementary to the great plants operated by the *zaibatsu*, to which they were usually in a position of complete dependency, many more supplied goods and services that had been in demand in Japan for centuries, and others were part of the complex of merchant-capital dominated activities which embraced many new consumption goods susceptible to small-scale production. There are many varieties of small-scale enterprise and it is no doubt dangerous to speak of 'the' problem of small-medium enterprise.[13] In this section we have been concerned merely with the effect of government policies in producing the small peak of the industrial pyramid.

2. The Structure of the Capital and Money Markets

If industrial structure is dual, the discovery that the organization of the capital market and the banking system is heavily in favour of big enterprise should not be surprising: the little man usually does find it more difficult to get accommodation. If this is true for most economies in most periods it is even more likely in a country which is forcing the pace of industrialization, and is seeking to establish strategic industries which require large amounts of capital. The banking system and channels of investment in Japan between 1870 and 1940 are often contrasted with the English banking system and capital market of the same period. But in the later nineteenth century the banking system in England was evolving into 'classical' commercial banking from earlier banking practices which much more closely resembled the Japanese, German, or American systems. Between the mid-eighteenth and mid-nineteenth centuries, English banks were more closely involved in financing industrial development—even the Bank of England bought railway debentures as early as 1842—and many banks crashed together with local firms in the frequent financial crises up to 1866. The difference between Japan from 1870 and England before the mid-nineteenth century lies in the evolution of banking from the industrial and commercial growth which took place in England over a long period: the involvement with industry was not so different but there was a tremendous disparity in resources. The English banks sprang from solid business growth in many areas, could therefore tap far wider sources, and in turn were able to provide far greater funds than the early Japanese banks.

As for the role of the capital markets in the two countries, it is probable that by the time the English banks were consciously adopting 'commercial' banking practices, this was possible not so much because the long-term capital market was sufficiently well-developed for the change to bring no inconvenience to English industrialists, as because demands on capital resources had shifted their emphasis. Until the 1870s Britain was not only engaged in the development of industries on a wide front, but was also providing the best infrastructure the world had yet seen. All this was a stupendous investment effort which sucked in all sections of the economy and caused great strains. Nevertheless it flowed from decades of growth and accumulation such as Japan had not enjoyed when she began to modernise in the 1870s. In a sense, it might be said that not only were Japan's banking structure and practices more appropriate to her needs, they were also not so very dissimilar from those in England in a period of English economic history which is more relevant for purposes of comparison.

Moreover, it could be argued that since the highly organised capital market in England was geared more to the needs of overseas investment and domestic public services than to the needs of manufacturing industry, it never, at any time in the nineteenth century, performed the function often attributed to it: that of supplying capital to domestic industrialists. These relied more on their own resources and those of personal contact than on the securities market, and up to the Macmillan Committee of 1931 and beyond there was never a shortage of complaints that industry was, in fact, ill-served by the highly developed capital and money markets, including banking, which England had boasted since the middle of

C

the nineteenth century. Nor has there been a lack of criticism of the failure to employ national capital resources for industrial modernisation at the turn of the century.

The course of events was quite different in late nineteenth century Japan from that in late nineteenth century England. The government took steps to mobilise capital for industry, surpluses from agriculture and taxes on consumers were channelled into the new sectors, and not only did the joint-stock banks become sources of funds for industrial investment, but special banks, such as the Hypothec Bank and the Industrial Bank of Japan, were created by the government to stimulate economic growth. The *zaibatsu* also gained from these developments, since as well as controlling the major commercial banks, they also exercised a great influence in the special financial institutions. The state thus played an important part in developing and controlling the institutions through which capital was supplied, in addition to its role in mobilising the sources of finance. As early as the spring of 1869 exchange companies were set up under the supervision of the Trade Bureau to perform some of the functions of joint-stock banks, and to work with the new trading companies which the government hoped would direct and stimulate both domestic and foreign commerce. In May and June, 1869, exchange companies were established in most of the major centres, and the most powerful partners in these firms were those, like Mitsui, Ono and Shimada who had been privileged exchange dealers in the Edo period.[14]

As in England, the course of banking history was far from smooth, but from these tentative and often unsuccessful beginnings,[15] the alliance of government and business groups built up a banking system which was geared directly to national aims. In just three decades, between 1872 and 1902, in addition to enacting laws providing for a commercial banking system and directly aiding the establishment of joint-stock banks, the government created the Bank of Japan, the Yokohama Specie Bank, the Hypothec Bank of Japan—together with forty-six prefectural industrial and agricultural banks—the Post Office Savings Bank and, finally, the Industrial Bank of Japan. Throughout, there was a sophisticated statement of policy. The preamble to the Industrial Bank of Japan Act of 1902 (*Nihon Kōgyō Ginkō-hō*) explained the government's aims:

> The demand for capital in Japan is great but the supply is inadequate. Therefore special financial institutions should be established to deal in negotiable securities such as shares and public bonds, and by maintaining real values of such securities, by

increasing confidence in them, and by facilitating their circulation, so to increase the supply of capital. . . .

The Industrial Bank's functions were to conduct trust business—to lend against securities, to underwrite public bonds, and so on.[16]
The Hypothec Bank was also designed to fill the gap left by the paucity of impersonal middle-class investors and for some years was an extremely important source of finance for both agriculture and industry.[17] By 1911 its debenture issues formed 53% of all bank debentures and although it later declined in importance one Japanese opinion is that it played a significant part in laying the foundations of the system of special banks and in the development of Japanese capitalism.[18] The Hypothec Bank acted as a kind of central bank for the prefectural Banks for Agriculture and Industry, buying their debentures and employing them as agents in making advances.[19]

These developments are remarkable not so much for the contrast to the English experience but for the echoes of Continental and American economic history. In the United States banking capital played a similarly direct role, and on the Continent special banks were extensively used. In Germany, Japan and the United States industrial concentration in the decades before the First World War was far more intense than in England; in all three countries banks were either founded by, or worked in close harmony with, the great industrial interests; and in all three countries there was much talk of the dominance of *Finanzkapital*.

Thus the pattern of evolution in Japan was by no means unique. It was, among other factors, the comparative gradualness of English economic development that produced its capital market and banking structures, structures which, it has often been assumed, should be repeated in other industrial economies. In fact, what happened in Japan was much closer to the general pattern of integration of financial and industrial capital in the industrialising economies of the West. And, even compared with England, the vacuum filled by the banks was not so much the lack of a public market for long-term investment in manufacturing—and there was certainly this gap in Japan—as the lack of capital accumulation by industry itself.

It is true that the telescoping of development in Japan gave an even greater impetus to financial and industrial concentration than in other countries, and there are other distinguishing characteristics which deepened the tendencies towards oligopoly. In Japan, unlike the western economies, the role of a public securities market and of imported capital in the development of utilities like railways was negligible. The state and the financial institutions therefore operated on an even wider front, and all this, with the government itself positively fostering concentration both in industry and in banking, resulted in big business dominating industry and finance to an unprecedented degree. The process was speeded up by episodes such as the crisis of 1901 and the subsequent failure of many small and medium-sized banks, and by government action to expand the scale of banking operations by forcing mergers and to prohibit the establishment of banks with small capitalisations.[20] Further, government determination to build a modern industrial and military power stimulated the concentration of economic power, not only directly by fostering the big concern and by forcing banking and industrial rationalisation, but indirectly through sheer technological necessity and the requirements of modern industrial organisation.

3. The Dependence on Imported Technology and Techniques

For the greater part of the nineteenth century, England epitomised advanced industrial technology and modern techniques of company and industrial organisation: her capital, machines, men, and know-how were exported not only to backward nations and colonies but also to advanced countries. Yet the latter—France, Germany, Belgium, the United States—made their own major contributions to technical, scientific, educational and organisational progress, and by the closing decades of the nineteenth century were rivalling England in many spheres. Moreover, their borrowings from England were spread over many decades and were absorbed into their own expanding corpus of technological knowledge; it was as early as 1779 that Frederick the Great of Prussia sent agents to Boulton & Watt's plant in Birmingham to copy Watt's atmospheric engine, and systematic study of new English machines, and employment of English technicians, was carried on by Prussia's administrators well into the nineteenth century.[21]

The stage of technological development reached by the industrial powers of the West posed a tremendous problem for Japan. True, she was a follower-nation as Prussia had been, but the gap in her case was immense by the 1870s. France, Prussia, the United States—these had grown, albeit more slowly, *with* as well as behind England, and by the time the Japanese emerged into the modern world there was not only a considerable degree of unity in western technology and education, shared by all these Western states, but also a great economic interdependence between the Atlantic economies. Japan shared practically none of this heritage and suffered under the additional handicap of being the kind of country the industrial powers were swallowing at will. So she had to catch up, and at the same time keep her independence; she had to adopt a vast range of new technology, and at the same time absorb new ideas and techniques of organisation. All this, without the benefit of the accumulation and experience enjoyed by even France and Germany.[22] In the industries needed to establish her as an industrial power comparable to her potential enemies, indivisibilities were great and increasingly great: railways, shipping, docks, ship-building, iron, steel, engineering and chemical plants, even textile plants, required capital outlays and technological know-how of daunting magnitudes for an economy based largely on agriculture. In addition, absorption of all kinds of new techniques of management, of commercial and company practice, and of industrial, social and political organisation was equally necessary. Foreign technicians were employed in pioneer enterprises right from the beginning of the Meiji period, and even before the Restoration Japanese were sent to all the major Western countries to study industry, commerce, finance, military systems, types of government and constitutions, and practically every aspect of Western life. By the early years of this century the foundations of the shipbuilding, heavy engineering, iron and steel, electrical power, electrical equipment and modern textile industries had been firmly laid, a railway system was being built up, and military forces had been successfully used in wars against China and Russia. All this was achieved largely from scratch and, in terms of concentrated effort bears comparison with Britain's industrial upsurge between 1770 and 1800, or Soviet Russia's between 1917 and 1945.

It is not surprising, therefore, that the nature of the industrial revolution in the West, a revolution which was already producing a world of giant combines, particularly in North America and Western Europe, should have had even more profound effects in Japan. Given the strategic necessity and the determination to introduce the industries of the West, the appropriate technology, all of which had to be imported, demanded large-scale operation which, in turn, called for financial resources to be concentrated. Hence the conjunction of the government, the banks, and a few great industrial concerns. Once established, the firms which received government contracts and subsidies, or had bought state-pioneered enterprises, or both, were inevitably placed in an overwhelmingly advantageous position. Whatever the motives of the government in selling off state enterprises in the early 1880's, one of the results was increased concentration of economic power. It was the *zaibatsu*, such as Mitsubishi, Mitsui, Sumitomo and Yasuda that particularly benefited and

emerged after the 1880s as great combines. They created banks themselves and increasingly cornered the supply of private capital, as well
as absorbing a large proportion of the capital channelled through
government organs. In the heavy industries this concentration was
necessary for the speedy development that was called for, and in
these industries, in coal, shipbuilding and steel, technological requirements made it extremely difficult for newcomers to establish themselves. Thus government policy, banking structure, the methods of
raising capital, and the technological requirements of the new
industrial era, interacted to enhance the trend towards concentration
of capital and industrial power seen in other countries. Already,
before the end of the nineteenth century, the pattern of the very big,
modern enterprise in the new industries was emerging in an economy
still characterised on the other hand by a multitude of small enterprises catering both for the great new companies, and also for the
'traditional' needs of the Japanese population.

4. The Consumption and Saving Habits of the Japanese

In any economy developing from a comparatively static and agricultural base there will be a mixture of new and traditional products.
Development is always uneven and areas of traditional consumption
and production will survive. It is often argued that if the traditional
sector refuses to give way growth is stunted: traditional social
groupings, traditional modes of thought, traditional craft techniques, and many other aspects of the old society must be eliminated
before new and rational methods can give their full fruit. In contrast
to this is the fear of the demonstration effect on the mass of the
people: the onslaught on traditional attitudes may be only too effective if it not only results in a willingness to leave the land, enter the
factory, and adopt more impersonalised relationships, but also leads
to demands for the fruits of the productivity made possible by the
new techniques. To stimulate new wants is to provide a spur to
growth; yet growth can only be rapid if the wants go largely unsatis-
fied.

It is a commonplace that in Japan this dilemma was seldom, if
ever, a serious problem in the period from 1870–1940. The country
managed to achieve a balance between modernisation and tradition-
alism that seems to have produced the ideal mixture for rapid growth.
There may well be grounds for believing that the achievements of
western capitalism 'depended upon its resting on top of a solid layer
of non-economic relationships',[24] and that, similarly, growth of the
modern sector in Japan rested upon a core of largely untouched

social and economic relationships, including consumption patterns which survived from the Tokugawa period:[25]

> The natural capability of the Japanese economy to mix the styles of its capital formation is one of the most important determinants of its successful growth. Japan brought to economic development a built-in resistance to the corroding influence of the demonstration effect—the deep commitment to a traditional economy that has continued to be productive to this day. The modern sector has succeeded because it climbed onto the shoulders of the traditional sector. . . . Two hundred years of isolation solidified a style of life until it could not be demolished, even by the powerful impact of an industrial revolution.

It was the government which received the demonstration effect and was determined to keep up with the Jones's, while the mass of the people were for decades insulated against many changes which usually accompany industrial growth, insulated with not only the apparatus of their past, but with new attitudes propagated by the state. The government was an important element in preserving this conservatism, as it was in most other spheres.

Since to some extent the dichotomy between large- and small-scale enterprise corresponds to the division between modern and traditional sectors, the persistence of traditional patterns of consumption, throughout decades of advancing heavy industry and manufacturing plants based on western methods of organisation, was a powerful cause of industrial dualism. To a great degree the markets for the two sections of industry were completely different, with government demand playing a conspicuous role in the large-scale sector, and the tremendously varied, fragmented demand from a population with traditional consumption habits rendering irrelevant the techniques of modern mass production. Particularly in housing, furniture, food, drink and dress were the markets varied and therefore narrow; they naturally dictated small-scale production. For some time after the Meiji Restoration the introduction of western products and techniques was largely confined to spheres which were not competitive with indigenous consumer industries, so there was no question of the widespread destruction of small-scale enterprises which has occurred in other economies. There are other elements in the survival of so much small-scale industry, such as the pattern of factor-endowment: even in new industries like bicycle and electric-bulb manufacturing, labour-intensive methods were used in preference to the latest techniques available in the West. Complementarity of large and small units in these and other industries existed early on and has earned admiring comment from many students of Japan, who have noted the ability of the Japanese to select as well as to imitate, and the successful combination of labour-intensive and capital-intensive in different branches of the same industry.[26] Thus it is in more than one way that modern industry can be said to have 'climbed onto the shoulders of the traditional sector': traditional and modern methods were mixed in new industries, and indigenous production survived in many spheres because of the strength of traditional patterns of consumption.

These consumption habits made a real contribution to the solution of the problem of holding down per capita consumption during early economic growth, and were thus a factor in the maintenance of high saving ratios, which early achieved levels comparable with the industrialised economies of the West, and which were impressively high if levels of per capita income are taken into account.[27] Much of the saving was, of course, quite involuntary, since it was enforced through the land tax, inflation, and sharply regressive consumer taxation (with heavy excise taxes on such items as sake, soya and sugar). Business and income taxes were for a time non-existent, and were then kept very low after their introduction. The resulting distribution of real income was therefore very favourable to economic growth in a society which accepted the strong centralised drive towards military and economic power, and which managed to remain satisfied with a comparatively unchanged pattern of private consumption.

Moreover, in spite of the large element of involuntary saving, individual savings in the lower income classes were substantial, a phenomenon which many have found intriguing and which must also be in part attributed to traditional consumption habits. The government added to customary thrift with its exhortations to save for *fukoku-kyōhei*. In view of the notorious reluctance of other peasant societies to place their savings in the hands of any financial institutions, let alone any sponsored by the government, the concentration of personal savings in banks, the post-office, and other organs for the small saver, was a striking achievement by the Meiji government. So in yet another way was the concentration of capital and industry fostered: the Japanese banks have long been noted for their willingness to attract myriads of tiny savers with a large variety of time-deposit accounts, and in the absence of direct investment opportunities this further enhanced the power of the banks and hence of the combines to which these belonged.

Thus both voluntary and involuntary savings were channelled

into big enterprise either via the government or via the banks. The high level of these savings depended on, among other things, the persistence of traditional consumption habits, which also ensured the survival of an extremely large sector of traditional production, production which was characterised by small-scale enterprise.

5. The Structure of the Labour Market and the Pattern of Agricultural Development

During the past century of economic development in Japan, the structure of the labour market has exerted a strong influence on industrial structure. More particularly, the increase in the working population had to be absorbed by the industrial, commercial and service sectors which, although they expanded very rapidly, were only barely equal to the task. These non-agricultural sectors included traditional industries, which therefore played an important part in maintaining employment and increasing output. Also interrelated in an obvious way are the large supplies of labour, and the existence of small industrial units in those modern sectors where such small units could be utilised by the big company. Certainly, the capital-intensive parts of the modern sector could absorb only a minor proportion of the increased labour force which resulted from the population explosion of the Meiji period.

From the 1870s to the 1930s, the working force in agriculture was extremely stable, although the population doubled, reaching seventy million in the mid-1930s. There was no devastating decline in the importance of agriculture such as occurred from the middle of the nineteenth century in Britain, where there was a significant *absolute* decline (of 38%) in numbers engaged, as well as a huge drop (from 22% to 6%) in *relative* employment between 1851 and 1931.[28] Some of the workers who could not be absorbed into agriculture or large-scale modern industrial plants in Japan went into small firms, connected with modern production, as suppliers of accessories and parts, but millions more entered commerce, distribution, personal service and craft trades: the sectors consisting predominantly of small units. While agriculture still engaged fourteen million in 1930 compared with about fifteen million in the early 1870s, the number of non-agriculturally employed rose from three million in 1872 to fifteen million in 1930.[29] Since employment in manufacturing rose by only four million in the same period, it is clear how important these other small-scale sectors were.

The labour market in pre-1940 Japan was therefore dominated by this great reservoir of labour pressing on non-agricultural employment opportunities. Great productivity increases in agriculture helped to maintain Japan's rapidly growing population and also provided surpluses for industrial growth. They were achieved without substantial changes in the social and economic structure of the countryside, which continued to absorb roughly the same number of people right up to the late 1930s. Thus Japanese economic development and structure have presented a rather unusual picture, one in which a growing industrial sector was combined with a large and stable agriculture, and in which this large and stable agricultural sector was capable of substantial gains in productivity while at the same time almost certainly harbouring a good deal of disguised unemployment. This has meant that there have, in the past, been reserves of labour available for periods of rapid industrial advance such as in the 1930s and 1950s, and also that the Japanese economy has had to find employment for millions who could find neither a place in agriculture, nor jobs in an industrial sector which was limited by the survival of consumption patterns that did not fit into the modern way of life and did not afford scope for the wider adoption of western modes of production.

The result was a labour market which was divided into two complementary but largely exclusive sections. The large modern companies developed systems of employment based on the selection of the best young workers for permanent jobs, permanent, that is, until the comparatively early retiring ages common in Japan. These workers would be taken straight from middle and high school, or from university, while most other employment sectors tapped the abundant sources of unskilled young, and the older skilled workers 'retired' from the big companies. Many of these older workers preferred to establish their own small enterprises, often producing or processing parts for their former employers. The very heavy reliance of big companies on subcontracting is an important feature of Japanese industrial structure, and Japanese economists, who are careful to point out that they are not unaware of the existence of subcontracting in other, more advanced, countries, insist that in Japan it rests on different economic and social foundations. Certainly it is true that it is difficult to find examples of parts-manufacturers being able to cause dislocation in Japanese industry, while this is far from uncommon in England.

The dual employment structure has been an integral part of the dual industrial structure and each has reinforced the other. The availability of large supplies of young labour—always desirable in times of rapid technological change because of its adaptability—enabled large companies to select and to adopt an employment structure which, once established, itself helped to perpetuate industrial dualism. The tendency of small units to proliferate was reinforced by the early retirement of skilled workers, and made possible by the large companies' willingness to give contracts to so many tiny, small, and medium sized units, either directly or indirectly through intermediaries.

III

These various factors overlapped and interacted in a way more intricate than their separation into five distinct forces implies.[30] The rise of the big companies—most of which were in the *zaibatsu*— the structure of the banking system and the capital market, the influence of technology and its wholesale importation from the West, the saving and consumption patterns, and the role of agriculture and the labour market, were all conditioned by one another, and were all overlaid by the policies of the Japanese government from the Meiji Restoration of 1868. The aim of these policies was a strong, independent Japan, capable of holding its own against the economic and military power of the Western nations. While it is true that changes were taking place before the Restoration, the developments in agriculture, industry and commerce, and reforms in administration, had not yet forged the kind of economic, social and political base from which England, for example, had sprung into the economic leadership of the world in the nineteenth century. Since Japan was under western pressure, rapid development was essential, and this accounted for the crucial role of the central government. Political and administrative developments in the Tokugawa period no doubt had direct and important effects on the subsequent pattern of bureaucratic and political control, but the speedy and effective centralization of power in the first decade of the Meiji era was very much a product of the reality of international power politics. The necessity for rapid economic growth also helped to determine the pattern of developments in capital, technology, agriculture and labour, developments which jointly produced the industrial structure which causes so much concern in Japan today. This industrial structure in turn reacted upon the other sectors as it became more firmly entrenched, while the natural tendency for traditional consumption habits to survive was powerfully reinforced by its elevation to a national virtue.

The strength of traditional attitudes and a mode of life which had become firmly established in the 250 years of isolation under

Tokugawa rule, together with the capital needs of a modern industrial sector in the technological and political setting of the later
nineteenth and twentieth centuries, ensured the development of a
dual industrial structure. The government, far from attacking the
concentration of economic power with anti-trust laws like those of
the United States, encouraged it with financial, fiscal and legislative
measures, so that by the 1930s the *zaibatsu* monopolised vast sectors
of the economy. In contrast to these combines, the bulk of the remainder of the economy was composed of millions of small enterprises. A large number of these were in commerce and service trades
which anywhere in the world are dominated by the small business.
But many were in industries which in other advanced countries
displayed a much smaller gap between the big and the small, in
productivity and wage levels, and in percentages of total employment. Not all of them catered for traditional consumption needs—
small enterprises had mushroomed round the big producers of
Western products—but many did, and in any case even those small
and medium businesses associated with the production of 'new'
products displayed the same characteristics which distinguished
them from their Western counterparts: much lower productivity and
income levels compared with larger companies, and an often overwhelmingly high degree of dependency as subcontractors. In spite
of the many changes since the end of the Second World War, in spite
of the outstanding record of economic growth, industrial dualism
is still a problem which causes a great deal of concern. In fact, it
could be argued that the pattern of growth since 1945 has borne such
a strong resemblance to that of the past that little alleviation of the
problem could be expected.

REFERENCES

1 Marius B. Jansen, *Sakamoto Ryōma and the Meiji Restoration*, Princeton,
1961, p. 347.
2 Fukushima Masao, 'Meiji shonen no keizai seisaku to shihon-chikuseki no
mondai' (Economic Policy in the Early Meiji Period and the Problem of Capital
Accumulation), *Tōyō Bunka*, No. 9, 1952, p. 3, reminds us that *fukoku-kyōhei*
were also the aims of the Tokugawa and han governments in the final years of
the old regime. But a strong, unified central government was needed to make the
policy effective, and this emerged only after 1868.
3 Cf. Miyashita Takehei, 'Zōsen kōgyō no hatten to kōzō' (The Development
and Structure of the Shipbuilding Industry) in Arisawa Hiromi (ed.), *Gendai
Nihon sangyō kōza* (Modern Japanese Industry), Vol. V: *Kikai kōgyō* (Machine
Industries), Pt. I, Tokyo, 1961, pp. 126–129.
4 Cf. Echigo Kazunori, *Nihon zōsen kōgyō-ron* (An Essay on the Japanese
Shipbuilding Industry), Tokyo, 1956, pp. 32–33.
5 Henry Rosovsky, *Capital Formation in Japan, 1868–1940*, Glencoe, Illinois,
1961, p. 23.

6 Tsuchiya Takao, *Nihon no seishō* (Political Merchants of Japan), Tokyo, 1956, p. 1.

7 Tsuchiya Takao, *Nihon keizai-shi* (An Economic History of Japan), Tokyo, 1963, p. 142.

8 G. C. Allen, *A Short Economic History of Japan, 1867–1937*, 2nd edn., London, 1962, Chapter VIII, is very useful on this topic.

9 Cf. T. C. Smith, *Political Change and Industrial Development in Japan: Government Enterprise, 1868–1880*, Stanford, 1955, pp. 85–100.

10 See the discussion in W. W. Lockwood, *The Economic Development of Japan: Growth and Structural Change, 1868–1938*, Princeton, 1954, Ch. X, which criticises the tendency to over-emphasise the role of the State.

11 T. C. Smith, *op. cit.*, contains a detailed study of the many new enterprises in non-traditional industries in Japan in this period.

12 Cf. Tatsumi Nobuharu, *Dokusen dankai ni okeru chūshō kigyō no kenkyū* (Studies of Small–Medium Enterprise in the Monopoly Stage [of Capitalism]), Tokyo, 1960, p. 247. See also Miyohei Shinohara, *Growth and Cycles in the Japanese Economy*, pp. 14–17.

13 An excellent discussion of industrial organization, which deals with many of the problems of small-scale enterprises in Japan in the 1930's may be found in G. C. Allen's massive contribution to E. B. Schumpeter, et al, *The Industrialization of Japan and Manchukuo, 1930–1940*, New York, 1940, pp. 476–786. The term 'small-medium enterprise' derives from the Japanese *chūshō-kigyō*.

14 Akashi Teruō and Suzuki Norihisa, *Nihon kinyū-shi* (A History of Japanese Finance), Tokyo, 1957, Vol. I, pp. 18–19.

15 In the early 1870's the habit of depositing in banks was, of course, still undeveloped, and the public is said to have regarded the first national banks (1872–1876) as 'loan-shops'—*kashikin toriatsukai-sho*. Cf. *Ibid.*, pp. 36–37.

16 Tsuchiya Takao, *Zoku Nihon keizai-shi gaiyō* (An Outline Economic History of Japan), Vol. II, Tokyo, 1939, p. 226.

17 Masahiro Fujita, 'The Banking System in the Middle Meiji Era (1870–1910), *Kobe Economic and Business Review*, No. 3, 1956, p. 77.

18 Itō Yuzuru, 'Kangin ruinen kashitsuke-daka no dōkō: keizai hatten to fudōsan ginkō' (Fluctuations in the Annual Advances of the Hypothec Bank: Economic Growth and the Mortgage Bank), *Nōgyō Keizai Kenkyū*, Vol. 24, No. 3, February 1953, pp. 19–20.

19 Masahiro Fujita, *op. cit.*, p. 61.

20 Tsuchiya Takao, *Keizai-shi gaiyō, op. cit.*, p. 227.

21 Cf. Fritz Redlich, 'The Leaders of the German Steam-Engine Industry During the First Hundred Years', *Journal of Economic History*, Vol. IV, No. 2, November 1944; and W. O. Henderson, 'Peter Beuth and the Rise of Prussian Industry, 1810–1845', *Economic History Review*, Sec. Ser., Vol. VIII, No. 2, December, 1955.

22 This is not to deny the relevance of stressing favourable circumstances like the spread of education and the existence of the 'samurai surplus' in pre-Restoration Japan. Cf. R. P. Dore, *Education in Tokugawa Japan* 1965, and G. C. Allen, 'Factors in Japan's Economic Growth', in C. D. Cowan (ed.), *The Economic Development of China and Japan*, London, 1964.

23 At times between one-half and two-thirds of the Ministry of Industry's total expenditure went on the salaries paid to foreign employees. Cf. Koichi Emi, *Government Fiscal Activity and Economic Growth in Japan, 1868–1960*, Tokyo, 1961, p. 115. As early as 1872 foreign employees of the Japanese government totalled 385: *ibid.*, p. 116.

24 V. A. Demant, *Religion and the Decline of Capitalism*, London, 1952, p. 29.

25 Rosovsky, *Capital Formation in Japan*, pp. 53 and 86.

26 See the discussion in Gustav Ranis, 'Factor Proportions in Japanese Economic Development', *American Economic Review*, Vol. XLVII, No. 5, September, 1957, pp. 599–602. Also the concluding remarks of Rosovsky and Ohkawa, 'The Indigenous Components in the Modern Japanese Economy', *Economic Development and Cultural Change*, Vol. IX, No. 3, April, 1961, who, however, note some negative aspects of the survival of indigenous components, or traditional industries, and suggest that they may now have outlived their usefulness.

27 Cf. Rosovsky, *Capital Formation in Japan*, p. 13.

28 Cf. Phyllis Deane and W. A. Cole, *British Economic Growth, 1688–1959*, Cambridge, 1962, pp. 142–143.

29 Tōbata Seiichi and Ohkawa Kazushi, *Nihon no keizai to nōgyō* (The Japanese Economy and Agriculture), Tokyo, 1962, Vol. I, p. 142.

30 Since this was written some important articles have been published on the pattern of Japanese economic development. See William W. Lockwood, *The State and Economic Enterprise in Japan: Essays in the Political Economy of Growth*, Princeton, 1965, particularly the essays by Professors Ohkawa and Rosovsky, and by Professor Landes. Also, T. Watanabe, 'Economic Aspects of Dualism in the Industrial Development of Japan', *Economic Development and Cultural Change*, Vol. XIII, No. 3, April, 1965.

CHAPTER 2

Economic Growth and Structure
after 1945

I

Between the two World Wars the Japanese economy had expanded, first under the influence of liberalism, then in the crisis-atmosphere of the 1930s, when economic and political nationalism grew more and more intense. The economy became even more orientated towards military build-up and heavy industry, and although the old *zaibatsu* suffered from political opposition and had to give some ground to new industrial groupings, the inroads made were slight and they remained very powerful indeed. The Allies were so convinced of the identity of militarism, authoritarianism, and economic oligarchy, that the destruction of the combines was a major part of their programmes of reform after the Japanese surrender of August 1945. It is therefore necessary to enquire in what sense post-war economic growth continued to display enough of the old pattern to justify the view that no substantial erosion of industrial dualism could be hoped for until the 1960s.

II

1. Labour and Agriculture

The Japanese economy was thrown back heavily on to the agricultural sector immediately after the Second World War. There were almost three million more people in agriculture in 1947 than in 1940, which meant that 50% of Japan's labour force depended on the land for their livelihood. Employment in manufacturing alone had dropped $1\frac{3}{4}$ million, and was still below the 1940 figure in 1955.[1] It is not surprising that many believed that Japan had permanently reverted to the status of an agricultural nation after a brief interlude of industrial expansion based on military aggression. But recovery was already under way: in 1947–1948 real gross national product rose by 10%, in 1948–1949 by over 16%, and although there was a sharp decrease in the growth rate in 1949–1950, the Korean War helped to boost the national product by over 12% per annum from 1950 to 1953.[2]

In the ten years after the end of the Korean War, Japan continued to expand her industry at a very rapid rate, placing such strong emphasis on the development of heavy industry that the word *jūkōgyō-ka* (heavy-industrialisation) came into use. The absolute size of agriculture and other primary employment began, in the later 1950s, to decline seriously for the first time. Agriculture by itself absorbed 50% of the labour force in 1947, which was, admittedly, a year of special difficulties; but in 1955 the proportion was still 38%, which was a very high percentage compared with other industrial nations. More impressive than the decline between 1947 and 1955, was the fall from 38% to 25%[3] which had occurred by 1962. These were the years of the great industrial boom in Japan: employment in manufacturing rose, and the labour force in primary production fell, by some two million.[4] Although this fall of two million was almost entirely in agriculture and therefore represents the first really serious decrease in the absolute size of the farming community, it still left rather more than thirteen million on the land, just about as many as found employment on both construction (2·7 million) and manufacturing (10·7 million) in 1962.[5]

So while agriculture has continued to feed the industrial labour force, it has remained very large. In Britain, for instance, agriculture absorbed little more than a million workers, or only 4% of employment, in 1961.[6] Since the growth in labour productivity has been far slower in agriculture than in manufacturing its relative contribution to national income has declined steeply, and this has seemed to justify the complaints that Japanese economic dualism is as strong as it ever was. In 1948 primary and secondary industries contributed almost exactly the same amount to the national income. The primary sector was in fact slightly in the lead, but in 1962 it produced only one-third of the income of the secondary sector. With an average productivity ratio of three to one in favour of secondary industry (in the most capital-intensive manufacturing industries the ratio is obviously much higher), and with the effects of the land reform, the attractions of urban industry have been strong. The push of land reform and the pull of modern industry can, perhaps, be separated as far as industrial structure is concerned. Productivity differentials within industry itself are so great that small and medium sized enterprises are likely to have benefited more from the push, although some rural areas are still so poor that there may even be a pull, while the big companies may have benefited more from the pull of higher wages.

At all events, the fact that Japan in the late 1940s and early 1950s had such an enormous rural population meant that both by population increase, and by the rundown of the agricultural labour force, urban industry had an abundant reservoir of labour. Indeed, as late as the mid-1950s many economists were convinced that it would be extremely difficult to cope with the growth in the national labour force. Negative or zero marginal productivity of labour was thought to exist in agriculture, which therefore harboured much latent unemployment. Population was increasing by over a million every year until the mid-1950s and the demographic pattern since the 1930s had been such that the size of the working-age group was increasing by almost exactly the same number. Between 1950 and 1960 total population and the fourteen to sixty-four age group each registered an increase of about ten million. In 1950 the working-age group was 61·4% of population, and in 1960 it was 65·9%.[7] What is noteworthy about this is not that this ratio was exceptionally high compared with other countries—in Britain the fifteen to sixty-four age group was 66% in 1955—but that it was increasing steadily, and that there was no serious unemployment, forecasts of which were common in the years before 1957. It was in this decade that Japan climbed into the top rank of industrial powers and displayed such spectacular progress in heavy and large-scale industry. Yet the importance of small-scale enterprises in terms of employment was hardly diminished at all by this growth of heavy industry.

Today this combination of great capital-intensive concerns and hundreds of thousands of small labour-intensive plants and businesses is condemned as an irrational survival of the past, as a typically 'Japanese' characteristic. Since the flow of fresh labour—either from the land or from population increase—has slackened off, the low productivity level of a very large proportion of the working force is becoming a real problem. But for much of the post-war period, as in the decades after the Meiji Restoration, the small and medium-sized businesses of Japan played an important role in the absorption of the millions who came on to the labour market. Furthermore, of the factors—outlined in Chapter 1—which determined the dual structure of industry, the supply of labour and the situation in agriculture were not the only ones to survive. Government policy, concentration on and in heavy industry, capital supply and industrial investment, and the continued reliance on foreign technology, all worked to perpetuate the dual structure. Even the old consumption habits have shown continued strength in some respects, although changes in this factor may now be much more important than any element of continuity.

2. Capital Formation and Industrial Investment

The capacity of the Japanese to discount the present has seemed, incredible even when compared with countries such as Norway where industrial expansion is extremely capital-intensive and is in any case based on an already high general standard of living. In 1960 they were willing to invest what has been called 'an almost unbelievable' proportion of their national product.[8] Yet the following year this proportion was pushed even higher, to over two-fifths. Ever

TABLE 2: *Gross Domestic Capital Formation in Japan, 1933–1962*

Fiscal Year	$\frac{GDCF}{GNP}$ %	Fiscal Year	$\frac{GDCF}{GNP}$ %	Fiscal Year	$\frac{GDCF}{GNP}$ %
1933	12·6	1943	24·9	1953	27·9
1934	18·0	1944	27·7	1954	23·4
1935	18·6	1945	—	1955	25·4
1936	20·2	1946	22·2	1956	31·8
1937	24·7	1947	26·4	1957	31·6
1938	23·7	1948	28·2	1958	27·3
1939	27·0	1949	24·6	1959	35·0
1940	26·8	1950	25·5	1960	38·2
1941	26·0	1951	30·6	1961	42·8
1942	26·9	1952	27·4	1962	37·2

Source: Keizai Kikaku-chō (Economic Planning Agency), *Kokumin shotoku hakusho Shōwa 37 nendo* (National Income White Paper for 1962–63), Tokyo, 1964, p. 123.

since the mid-1930s there has been a secular trend towards ever-greater investment, and the ratios became exceptionally high when war with China grew more intense from 1939. But even the high figures of the Second World War lose their impact when compared with those since 1950. In 1951, for the first time, investment was 30% of gross national product. This was, of course, the first full year of the Korean War and may therefore be regarded as exceptional. Certainly there was a subsequent decline, but in 1955 the Japanese economy began a new phase of its expansion.

Since 1956 the proportion of gross national product invested has only once fallen below 30% and the average proportion in the four years from 1959–1962 was 38%. It was in these years, it may be recalled, that the growth rate of the economy jumped to average 15% per annum,[9] and that Western countries like Britain and France found themselves ousted from their positions as producers of steel, commercial vehicles, cement, and other key items. If the industrial and financial structures built up between 1870 and 1940 had been conducive to the rapid expansion of heavy industry they were, in alliance with a government still prepared to encourage and stimulate, even more favourable in the circumstances of the 1950s.

Capital formation in industry in general, and in a comparatively few industries in particular, took a lion's share of this huge and ever-increasing investment: investment ratios were, remember, increasing when gross national product itself was growing at a very fast rate. First of all, the proportion of gross private capital formation which went into fixed industrial investment grew rapidly (see Table 3) in

TABLE 3: *Composition of Gross Private Domestic Capital Formation in Japan, 1946–1962* (%)

Fiscal Year	GPDCF	Producers' Durables	Residential Construction	Inventories
1946	100	49·2	14·0	36·8
1947	100	47·5	11·1	41·4
1948	100	42·8	9·5	47·7
1949	100	54·2	6·7	39·1
1950	100	47·7	7·3	45·0
1951	100	48·7	5·7	45·6
1952	100	59·2	8·0	32·8
1953	100	60·0	9·5	30·5
1954	100	65·7	11·5	22·8
1955	100	56·7	10·4	32·9
1956	100	60·6	8·7	30·7
1957	100	70·5	9·3	20·2
1958	100	86·7	12·4	0·9
1959	100	66·0	8·4	25·6
1960	100	71·9	8·0	20·1
1961	100	69·7	7·7	22·6
1962	100	77·4	10·9	11·7

Source: See Table 2, p. 30: Keizai Kikaku-chō, *op. cit.*, pp. 150–151.

the 1950s and early 1960s: usually less than 50% in the years up to 1951 it ranged from 61% to 87% between 1956 and 1962. Private residential construction never absorbed more than 12% after 1946 and, generally speaking, was extremely low compared with such investment in the United States, West Germany and Britain. Between 1950 and 1957 the proportions ranged from 19% to 31% in the U.S.A., from 15% to 25% in Britain, and from 36% to 45% in West Germany.[10] In Japan the range was from 6% to 12%, which does not surprise anyone familiar with her low housing standards.

A special characteristic of capital formation in Japan has been the very high investment in stocks, but even this began to succumb to the boom in producers' durables and to improvement in distribution and from 1956 it absorbed a much lower proportion of investment. This decline, and the suppression of investment in housing, have combined with the relative fall in personal consumption and the containment of government expenditure to make possible the huge increase in fixed capital formation in industry. The following figures in Table 4 show both the relative fall in consumption and the steady, even decreasing, proportion of national expenditure which has been taken by government for its outlay on goods and services. Personal consumption was bound to take a high proportion of the national product in the early post war years, when there was widespread poverty, but the relative decline was greater than any return to normal pre-war levels warranted. Between 1930 and 1936 the proportion consumed never fell below 65%, while from 1950–1962 it never rose above that figure. In the same pre-war period government's share ranged between 12 and 17%, but since the war the proportion has, on average, been considerably lower and has never once reached the minimum pre-war figure.[11] Both the ratios of consumption and government expenditure on goods and services are considerably lower in Japan than in most advanced Western nations.

What impressed many observers about this gigantic feat of saving, was the almost single-minded concentration in the years between 1946 and 1956 on a few industrial sectors which were given an overwhelming priority for investment funds. Coal, electricity, marine transportation, and iron and steel were singled out for rapid expansion by both the government and the banks, which were under pressure from the government to adopt this leading policy. A good illustration of this concentration of investment is that in the four years from 1949–1952, 90% of the funds allocated from the Counterpart Fund for fixed investment in private industry went to these four sectors.[12] They also absorbed 43% of all loans made for fixed

TABLE 4: *Consumption, Investment, and Government Expenditure in Japan, 1946–1962* (%)

Fiscal Year	Gross National Expenditure		
	Personal Consumption	*Total Investment**	*Govt. Expend. on Goods & Services*
1946	70·3	22·2	11·6
1947	69·9	26·4	7·8
1948	65·3	28·2	10·6
1949	67·0	24·6	11·7
1950	60·7	25·5	11·1
1951	55·4	30·6	10·1
1952	60·1	27·4	11·2
1953	61·4	27·9	10·9
1954	63·5	23·4	11·4
1955	62·1	25·4	10·8
1956	59·2	31·8	10·1
1957	58·9	31·6	10·1
1958	60·5	27·3	10·3
1959	54·7	35·0	9·4
1960	52·4	38·2	9·2
1961	50·3	42·8	8·9
1962	53·1	37·2	9·6

* Includes government investment.

Source: See Table 2, p. 30: Keizai Kikaku-chō, *op. cit.*, p. 123. The annual totals of the three items vary above or below 100% according to movements in the net balance of foreign claims.

investment by the commercial banks to every branch of enterprise, including agriculture, over much the same period.[13] The Japan Development Bank devoted 84% of its total loans to the 'Big Four'— as these industries came to be called—in the years 1951–1955, by which time both the need and the effort began to slacken off. Between 1956 and 1962 the proportion dropped to 69%, which, however, was by no means an insignificant figure. Over the whole period 1951–1962, 74% of the Bank's funds for investment went to these four industries.[14]

From 1956 other industries began to attract more attention: ship-building had already achieved world primacy in launchings, and the chemical, electrical equipment, petroleum and automobile industries were giving a new look to the Japanese economy while at the same time adding to its degree of 'heavy-industrialisation'. In addition, investment in steel and electricity was maintained at high levels, although coal and shipping were giving way to rail and road transport, and to petroleum. Table 5 shows the share of total fixed investment received by major industries in each of the years from 1951–1962. The figures clearly show the structural changes which have given Japan such a powerful industrial economy since the mid-1950s: investment proportions in mining, shipping, electricity, agriculture and textiles roughly halved, machinery and chemicals doubled their share, while iron and steel moved on to a higher plateau. As we shall see, even government spokesmen have linked this pattern of investment, which has been strongly influenced by government policy, to the problem of economic and industrial dualism. There has been tacit admission that the emphasis on heavy industry—and the big company—has led to some neglect of other sectors of the economy, with too little being done to alleviate the unfortunate aspects of industrial structure.

3. Industrial Concentration

The attempt under the Allied Occupation to break up the industrial combines after the war was not wholly unsuccessful. But the early emphasis on investment in mining and shipping and other heavy sectors, coupled with the traditionally powerful position of the great city banks, inevitably produced an industrial and financial pattern which closely resembled the old system. Even Mitsui, the *zaibatsu* said to have been most adversely affected by dissolution, necessarily gained in the process—it had long been prominent in mining—and its decline compared with Mitsubishi is more likely due to its relative failure to expand into the growth industries of the 1950s. Mitsubishi certainly is still a very powerful name in most branches of modern engineering and constructional activity, operations which are backed by Mitsubishi banks and investment trusts, and there are now over thirty Mitsubishi companies, some of which are extremely large.

These companies, like those of other *zaibatsu*, remained formally separate for some years but have recently moved towards a more centralized control. For instance, three of the largest Mitsubishi engineering companies, which were formed in 1950 after the dissolution of Mitsubishi Heavy Industries Ltd under the Enterprise

TABLE 5: *Distribution of Fixed Investment in Japan, 1951–1962* (%)

Industry	Fiscal Year											
	1951	1952	1953	1954	1955	1956	1957	1958	1959	1960	1961	1962
Mining	7	8	6	5	5	3	4	4	3	3	3	3
Shipping	15	12	7	6	7	7	8	6	4	3	2	3
Electricity	13	21	24	27	25	20	19	23	18	16	13	14
Iron & Steel	8	8	6	5	4	6	9	9	11	11	11	9
Sub-total	*43*	*49*	*43*	*43*	*41*	*36*	*40*	*42*	*36*	*33*	*29*	*29*
Machinery	5	7	7	6	5	8	10	9	11	15	17	14
Chemicals	10	7	7	8	8	10	12	10	11	13	14	13
Sub-total	*15*	*14*	*14*	*14*	*13*	*18*	*22*	*19*	*22*	*28*	*31*	*27*
Textiles	13	5	7	7	7	10	5	4	5	4	4	4
Agriculture*	10	11	11	12	13	8	6	5	5	6	6	6
Non-Marine Transport	6	4	7	6	5	7	6	6	6	7	7	8
Other	13	17	18	18	21	21	21	24	26	22	23	26
Total	100	100	100	100	100	100	100	100	100	100	100	100

* Includes forestry and fisheries.

Source: Nihon Kaihatsu Ginkō Chōsa-bu (Research Division of the Japan Development Bank), *Chōsa geppō* (Monthly Bulletin), Vol. 12, Nos. 4–5, July, 1963, Table 3, following p. 102.

Reorganization and Readjustment Law, merged again in June 1964 to form a company which is rivalled only by Hitachi in Japan.[15] The government, far from providing such deterrents as the British Monopolies Commission's spotlight, is demanding mergers in many branches of industry. There is a strong belief that success in international competition goes to the great, diversified company or to an industry which is prepared drastically to reduce the number of its members. Moreover, threats are made—to the shipping companies, for instance—that if there are no mergers government support will not be forthcoming. All this pressure is exerted under the clarion call to merge and rationalise to make Japanese industry an effective part of the 'open economy' to which the country is committed under its GATT, OECD and IMF membership.

One measure of the predominance of the *zaibatsu* before their formal dissolution is the percentages of paid-up capital they commanded in the various financial, commercial and industrial sectors.[16] As Table 6 shows, the four biggest *zaibatsu* alone controlled half of financial capital, a third of the capital in heavy industry and almost two-thirds of the capital in the shipping industry. Apart from their overwhelming strength in finance, they were particularly strong in mining, machinery and machine tools, chemical and ceramics production. In the 1930s they were joined in these latter fields by some smaller *zaibatsu*, but these groups never achieved anything like the same importance in finance, which was a very crucial factor in the ability of the older *zaibatsu* to expand into new fields. When we add the two groups of *zaibatsu* together the prevalence of the term *dokusen shihon*—monopoly capital—in Japanese economic literature becomes understandable: the ten *zaibatsu* commanded over one-third of all paid-up capital in all sectors.

In terms of paid-up capital the power of the big four *zaibatsu* was relatively lower in 1960 than it had been in 1946. It was then estimated that they controlled 544 companies and 25% of paid-up capital, while in 1960, 120 companies with 16% of the total capital were considered to be under their control.[17] But these figures are also evidence of the growing size of individual *zaibatsu* companies and, moreover, we must bear in mind the increased importance of bank credit in the 1950s compared with the pre-war position. Since the role of banks and trust companies in financing industrial investment is very great, and since individual *zaibatsu* banks retain close links with the many companies previously controlled by the *zaibatsu* holding companies, there is a considerable concentration of financial and industrial power. It has been estimated that in March 1958 the banks, trusts, insurance and securities companies belonging to Mitsui Mitsubishi, Sumitomo and Fuji (previously Yasuda), controlled

TABLE 6: *Capitalisation of Zaibatsu Companies before Dissolution* (% *of Total Paid-Up Capital*)

Sector		Zaibatsu		
		Big Four (a) % of Total	Smaller Six (b) % of Total	Ten Zaibatsu % of Total
Finance	Banking	48	2	50
	Trusts	85	—	85
	Insurance	51	9	60
Sub-total		50	3	53
Heavy Industry	Mining	28(c)	22	51(d)
	Metals	26	15	42
	Machinery	46	22	68
	Shipbuilding	5	8	13
	Chemical	31	7	39
Sub-total		32	17	49
Light Industry	Paper	5	—	5
	Ceramics	28	27	56
	Textiles	17	1	19
	Others	6	7	13
Sub-total		11	6	17
Miscell- aneous	Shipping	61	1	61
	Real estate, Building & Storage	23	7	29
	Commerce & Foreign Trade	14	7	20
	Others	2	—	2
Sub-total		13	3	16
Totals—all sectors		25	11	35

NOTES:

(a) The big four *zaibatsu* were Mitsui, Mitsubishi, Sumitomo, and Yasuda.

(b) The smaller six *zaibatsu* were Aikawa, Asano, Furukawa, Ōkura, Naka-jima, and Nomura.

(c) This figure is incorrectly given as 38 in the source cited below.

(d) Discrepancies in totals are the result of rounding to the nearest per cent.

Source: Ikeuchi Nobuyuki, *op. cit.*, p. 17.

36% of the resources of all financial institutions.[18] It is also calculated that of the 360 largest companies in Japan, over one-third are in
these four groups, while over one-half are in the six groups of
Mitsubishi, Mitsui, Sumitomo, Fuji, Daiichi and Sanwa.[19]

Big business has become bigger in Japan as in other countries,
such as West Germany, Britain, and the United States. The movement has been particularly strong in Germany and Japan, and the
view is increasingly taken that other countries must follow their
example if they are to succeed in international markets. For instance,
France is said to be weak in this respect and has only twenty-five of
the world's top companies (excluding the U.S.A.) compared with
Japan's thirty-seven.[20] In 1958 Japan boasted only four of the world's
top hundred companies (again excluding the U.S.A.) but by 1961
this number had increased to fourteen.[21].

Not all the great industrial companies of Japan depend on affilia-
tions with the old *zaibatsu*. But some companies, like Hitachi, which
emerged from dissolution have become so huge that one is tempted
merely to add a couple of new names to the list of *zaibatsu* to sum up
industrial concentration since the end of the Occupation. The
domination of the economy by a few groups had reached an almost
fantastic degree by 1945 and it is, perhaps, unlikely that this concentration could go so far a second time. But the financial centres of
industrial groups—the banks and finance companies of Mitsui,
Mitsubishi, Sumitomo, Fuji, Daiichi, and Sanwa, particularly—
are now so strong that they have a head start in any new sphere of
production. It is true that some of these financial nuclei are less
closely bound to particular industrial concerns than others, but all
are involved in industrial and financial structures which are inter-
locked to a degree quite foreign to British concepts. This structure
has, with the stimulation of government policy and rapid technological change, canalised credit and other resources to the benefit
of the companies in the big combines. As they grow they gather
around themselves a host of lesser enterprises, which range in size
from the tiny firm of a handful of workers to the medium-large plant
of between 300 and 1000 employees. These firms are often completely
dependent on the big companies not only for orders, but for skilled
personnel, working capital, fixed capital, and technological expertise.

4. Industrial Change: The Growth of Heavy Industry, 1946–1962

Table 7 shows how successfully the Japanese have pursued their
goal of 'heavy-industrialisation', how energetically they have transformed the image of their economy from one of toys, pretty tea-sets,

TABLE 1. *Composition of Industrial Production in Japan 1946–1962 (%)*

Commodity	Fiscal Year										
	1946	1949	1952	1955	1956	1957	1958	1959	1960	1961	1962
Iron & Steel	5·0	8·7	8·8	10·5	10·5	10·0	9·3	9·7	12·5	13·2	11·9
Non-ferrous Metals	3·7	3·3	2·6	3·9	3·8	3·5	3·4	3·5	3·4	3·1	3·1
Machinery	23·3	24·0	21·8	19·9	23·4	27·4	29·2	33·2	34·0	36·4	36·9
Chemical	10·3	12·0	12·5	12·6	12·4	12·2	12·6	10·7	9·0	8·6	9·3
Petro-chemical*	1·1	1·2	2·3	2·2	2·3	2·3	2·4	2·4	1·9	1·9	2·0
Heavy Industry sub-total	*43·4*	*49·2*	*48·2*	*49·1*	*52·4*	*55·4*	*56·9*	*59·6*	*60·8*	*63·2*	*63·2*
Ceramics	4·3	5·0	4·4	5·7	5·7	5·6	5·3	4·9	3·7	3·6	3·7
Textiles	23·9	22·3	26·7	17·5	17·0	15·8	14·1	13·1	12·2	11·0	10·9
Food	13·7	10·5	8·1	13·4	11·5	10·0	10·8	9·0	9·1	8·4	8·2
Other	14·7	13·0	12·8	14·3	13·4	13·2	12·9	13·4	14·2	13·8	14·0
Light Industry sub-total	*56·6*	*50·8*	*51·8*	*50·9*	*47·6*	*44·6*	*43·1*	*40·4*	*39·2*	*36·8*	*36·8*
All Industries Total	100	100	100	100	100	100	100	100	100	100	100

* Includes chemical by-products from coal.

Sources: 1946–1959: Kotani Chiaki, *Nihon no kōgyō shihon* (Industrial Capital in Japan), Tokyo, 1960, p. 11.
1960–1962: Keizai Shingikai (Economic Deliberation Council), *Kokumin shotoku baizō keikaku chūkan kentō hōkoku* (Report on the Interim Study of the National Income Doubling Plan), Tokyo, 1964, pp. 186–187.

and cheap textiles, to one of steel, machinery, ships and chemicals. Once again the figures show the structural water-shed of the mid-1950s: in 1955 light industry accounted for 50% of total industrial output but this proportion decreased rapidly down to 1962 when it provided only 37%. Textiles' share more than halved, while iron and steel, and machinery, took up most of heavy industry's 63%. This was the result of a conscious policy of concentrating investment resources on the branches of industry in which Japan saw a hopeful future for exports, or which were necessary as basic utilities. Steel and machinery absorbed 23% of fixed investment in 1962 compared with 9% in 1955.[22] For decades the Japanese steel industry had been a weak link, but between 1955 and 1961 its production trebled to $28\frac{1}{4}$ million tons, which was the world's fourth largest output,[23] and which provided a firm domestic base for the great expansion of the machine industries. The latter accounted for 37% of industrial output in 1962, and it is difficult to imagine how such sectors as ship-building and commercial vehicle production could have expanded so rapidly without the sharp rise in domestic steel production.

The Japanese government was not in any way an authoritarian planner in this period, but it contributed help, approval, and pressure in moving the economy towards the goals laid down in successive economic plans. These plans persistently underestimated the growth potential of the Japanese economy, but they also consistently advo-cated restriction of consumption and the promotion of both private and government investment policies which concentrated on heavy industry. Government and individuals, companies and workers, banks and savers—the efforts of all should be geared 'to channel necessary funds into basic industries which are the pillars for the achievement of the goal of economic growth'.[24] Throughout the years since the end of the Occupation, the economic surveys and the economic plans have shown a constant preoccupation with compari-sons of Japanese and Western industrial structures. Transformation of Japan's structure has been sought to achieve an 'international level of industrialisation' which, as Table 8 shows, Japan quickly attained after the mid-1950s. If the definition of heavy industry is restricted to metals and machinery she had outstripped other leading countries by 1961.

While the upward trend in Germany, Italy and Japan is clear, Britain appears to have been on a plateau since about 1955 (with dips in the percentage in 1956 and 1958, which are not shown in Table 8), and the share of metals and machinery in the United States dropped after 1957. However, all five countries show a substantial relative increase in heavy industrial production compared with the 1930s,

TABLE 8: *Heavy Industrial Production* as a Proportion of Total Industrial Production* (%)

	1938	1948	1951	1955	1957	1959	1961
United States	24	37	39	41	41	39	39
Britain	36	44	44	47	47	47	48
West Germany	37	30	33	39	39	40	42
Italy	—	—	—	35	36	35	37
Japan	20	33	33	32	39	44	50

* Iron and steel, non-ferrous metals, and machinery.

Source: Namiki Nobuyoshi in *Nihon keizai no jūkōgyō-ka* (The Heavy Industrialisation of the Japanese Economy), Tokyo, 1964, p. 10. The *Economic Survey of Japan* (*1961–1962*), p. 244 puts the British figure at 47 and the Japanese figure at 54 for 1961, but Namiki's figures are revised estimates, using indices with different base years.

and if chemical production is included the figures for both Britain and the United States, as well as for other Western countries, confirm the Japanese view that it is in metals, machinery and chemicals that the key to economic and international competitive power lies. With this index as a basis for comparison Japan's advance is still striking, but Britain, the United States, West Germany and France all experienced substantial and similar shifts in industrial structure:

TABLE 9: *Proportion of Heavy and Chemical Production in Total Industrial Production* (%)

	Japan	U.S.A.	W. Germany	Britain	Sweden	France	Italy
1953	48·3	55·1	46·7	55·3	47·3	50·3	53·4
1959	57·7	57·2	52·7	60·8	47·9	57·6	60·4
1961	63·2	62·5	63·8	62·6	49·9	71·8	55·9

Source: Keizai Shingikai (Economic Deliberation Council), *op. cit.*, p. 196.

Thus it is in this wider group of industries that Japan has seen, and met, her principal challenge. According to almost all the indices she is one of the giants of the industrial world. But, to revert to page 3 of this essay, her economic structure still stimulates profound dissatisfaction. To the Japanese, parity of heavy industrial and chemical production compared with total industrial output is not enough: their country is still below the most advanced nations when industrialisation is compared with the entire national economy. In fact, the authors of the Interim Study of the National Income Doubling Plan insist, she just cannot rank as an advanced nation. They quote the following figures to prove it:

TABLE 10: *Heavy Industrial Production as a Proportion of Net National Income* (%)

	Japan	U.S.A.	Britain	W. Germany	France	Italy
1950	8·8	14·8	16·5	13·2	17·6	10·2
1955	7·7	16·5	21·0	17·5	16·7	11·4
1960	14·4	15·4	17·8	18·4	18·9	13·6

Source: See Table 9: Keizai Shingikai, *loc. cit.*

Obviously it is the three north-western European countries which are the yardstick here: economic structure in the United States, for all its great wealth, reflects severe problems, while Italy is precisely what Japan is—a dual economy. The large and comparatively poor agrarian sector, and the problem of industrial dualism, have become, it is believed in Japan, the biggest obstacles to placing the country once and for all on a par with the most advanced industrial nations of the world. They are responsible for what is regarded as the poor showing in Table 10 and, as a corollary, for the extremely low position Japan occupies in the international league of *per capita* incomes. It is sometimes said that the low *per capita* figures are a puzzling and misleading contradiction of the evident and widespread prosperity of the Japanese, and it is argued that the purchasing power of Japanese incomes is underrated. But, as in the United States and in Italy, there are still substantial sections of the population which do not enjoy the same standards as the mass of the urban population. Furthermore, housing and social amenities are still backward, and there remains, as many Japanese see it, a large residue of truth in the belief that Japan must now turn, and turn with great energy, to the solution of the problems of duality both in the economy at large, and within industry itself.

III

We have traced the continued influence of agricultural structure, of the pattern of capital formation and concentration of capital supplies, of the strength of industrial groupings, and last, but not least, of active state encouragement and pressure for a pattern of industrial development which has not, it is generally agreed, eliminated the problems of industrial dualism. We now turn to Part II of this essay, which attempts to give a more precise picture of what is meant by industrial dualism in Japan, and which seeks to estimate the extent to which the constantly reiterated government pledges to eradicate the dual structure in industry are reflected in the statistics of dualism.

REFERENCES

1 Institute of Economic Research, Hitotsubashi University, *Annotated Economic Statistics of Japan*, Tokyo, 1961, p. 40. This volume is in Japanese, apart from the title and list of contents.

2 See Keizai Kikaku-chō (Economic Planning Agency), *Kokumin shotoku hakusho Shōwa 37 nendo* (National Income White Paper for 1962–63), Tokyo, 1964, p. 163 for these growth rates.

3 Including forestry, fisheries and mining.

4 These figures are from Tsūshōsangyō Daijin Kambō Chōsa-tōkei-bu (Research and Statistical Section of the Secretariat of the Minister for International Trade and Industry), *Tsūshōsangyō tōkei yōran Shōwa 38 nen* (Statistical Survey of Trade and Industry for 1963), Tokyo, 1963, pp. 12 and 316.

5 Division of Labor Statistics and Research, Ministry of Labor, Japan, *Year Book of Labor Statistics 1962*, Tokyo, 1964, Table 5, pp. 12–13.

6 National Economic Development Council, *Growth of the United Kingdom 1961–1966*, London, 1963, p. 23.

7 1950 figures from *Annotated Economic Statistics of Japan, op. cit.*, p. 38. 1960 figures calculated from Bureau of Statistics, Office of the Prime Minister, *Japan Statistical Yearbook 1962*, Tokyo, 1963, Table 10, p. 24 and Table 23, pp. 44–45.

8 Rosovsky and Ohkawa, 'Recent Japanese Growth', *op. cit.*, p. 583.

9 See above, p. 4.

10 *Annotated Economic Statistics of Japan, op. cit.*, p. 15.

11 All these figures are from the source cited on p. 30, Table 2.

12 Ikeuchi Nobuyuki, *Kigyō shūchū-ron* (An Essay on Business Concentration), Tokyo, 1964, p. 117. The Counterpart Fund was derived from the sale of American aid to Japan.

13 *Ibid.*, p. 118. That is, 43% of the difference between loans outstanding at the end of fiscal 1948 and at the end of fiscal 1951.

14 Nihon Kaihatsu Ginkō Chōsa-bu (Research Division of the Japan Development Bank), *Chōsa geppō* (Monthly Bulletin), Vol. 13, No. 1, April, 1964, p. 65. All years are fiscal years.

15 The merger has been called 'a monumental event' in the strengthening of Japanese monopoly capital: Misonou Hitoshi, 'Nihon dokusen shihon no kyōka toteichaku' (The Strengthening of Monopoly Capital in Japan), *Keizai Hyōron*, May, 1964, p. 11.

16 Concrete measures to dissolve the holding companies, were not taken until October, 1946. For a detailed study of the attempt to break up the zaibatsu see T. A. Bisson, *Zaibatsu Dissolution in Japan*, Berkeley, 1954.

17 Ikeuchi Nobuyuki, *op. cit.*, p. 73.

18 Nagasu Kazuji, *Nihon keizai nyūmon* (An Introduction to the Japanese Economy), Tokyo, 1960, p. 124.

19 See the figures given in Ikeuchi, *op. cit.*, p. 72, and Nagasu, *op. cit.*, pp. 122–123.

20 Cf. *The Times*, 8 October, 1964.

21 Ikeuchi Nobuyuku, *op. cit.*, p. 78.

22 See above, Table 5, p. 35.

23 *Japan Statistical Yearbook 1963*, Tokyo, 1964, Table 92, p. 164.

24 Cf. Economic Planning Agency, Japanese Government, *New Long-Range Economic Plan of Japan* (*FY 1958–FY 1962*), Tokyo, n.d., pp. 14–19, for these views.

PART II

INDUSTRIAL DUALISM AND ECONOMIC POLICY IN JAPAN

CHAPTER 3

The Scale of Industry

and

Recent Economic Policy

I

If the superlatively rapid economic growth of the 1950s and early 1960s produced some of the world's greatest industries and giant companies in Japan, it still left problems of industrial structure which one Cabinet Minister termed 'the heavy burden of the Japanese economy',[1] and which seemed so important to another that he insisted that the co-operation of the entire population was necessary if they were to be solved.[2] Occasionally a George Schwartz of Japanese journalism reflects a widespread cynicism about politician's motives, and asks why it is so strange to find big and small in industry and commerce, but generally speaking the newspapers treat the problem of industrial dualism as seriously as do academic economists. Leading Japanese newspapers carried references to the problem almost every day in the autumn of 1963 (which was General Election time) and the winter and spring of 1964 (which was a period of tight money and multiplying bankruptcies).

At the same time Japanese economists were adding to the already huge list of books and articles on the *chūshō kigyō mondai*—the problem of small-medium enterprise—and their doyen in this field, Professor Tokutarō Yamanaka, provided an introduction to a volume on *Economic Growth and the Smaller Enterprise* in which he reiterated his view that this problem is a special one for Japan. Certainly other countries—even high income ones like the United States and Britain— have their small-scale businesses but these occupied a much bigger part of Japan's economic structure, and were characterised by the closely interlocking and undesirable contradictions of low productivity, low wages, low technological levels, and excessive competition. The problem was not only a labour problem and a social problem; it was, in view of the gap in fixed assets, value-added, and incomes, a problem of business economics and of economic policy.[3]

47

An immense array of statistics is used in the discussion of large and small-scale industry, and there are many pitfalls, such as the confusion between plant and enterprise,[4] but even in general terms the figures can be very illuminating. The problem may be approached from various standpoints: the national economy, the scale in secondary and tertiary sectors as a whole, the prevalence and characteristics of small-scale enterprise in secondary industry only, and finally the scale-structure within particular industries. In the national economy agriculture still has a comparatively large, though declining, weight, and it is, of course, overwhelmingly small-scale. Agriculture was considered in Part I of this essay for the role it has played, and still plays, in Japanese economic development, but this wider aspect of the dual economy is not our primary concern here. We come closer to the problem in manufacturing industry when we look at the tertiary sector, because it is here—perhaps even more than in agriculture—that there is scope for changes which would aid the drive towards a more efficient economy. Thus although we are mainly interested in dualism in secondary industry, it is of considerable interest first to survey the extent of small-scale enterprise in the entire non-agricultural sector.

It is no surprise to see from Table 11 that, by number, smaller businesses are overwhelmingly predominant in industrial sectors as well as in agriculture. Although the figures are a little extreme by international standards, they are not so very different in most sectors from those in Britain and the United States. It is in the employment statistics, and in the huge size of distribution, that the interest lies. Two-thirds of Japan's industrial and commercial labour force work in small- and medium-sized businesses. Particularly impressive are the high proportions in the biggest sectors: distribution (79%), manufacturing (62%), services (76%), and construction (86%). These proportions are high by international standards: in the United States, for instance, manufacturing concerns with fewer than 250 employees absorbed only 43% of the total work-force in manufacturing in 1958, compared with 62% in Japanese concerns with fewer than 300.[5] Since the crux of the Japanese problem lies in the large productivity differentials between large and small-scale firms, the distribution of manpower is unfavourable even in the manufacturing sector, and this constitutes one of the many tasks facing the country.

The situation is even worse in distribution. Naturally one expects retail shops to be small—hence the different criterion for measuring smallness. A more precise understanding of the problem in this, as in other, sectors depends on a more detailed analysis of scale, but for

TABLE 11. *Industrial Distribution of Enterprises and Employment, and Proportion of Smaller Enterprises in Japan*

Industry	No. of Enterprises (1960)			Employment (000) (1962)		
	Total (A)	Smaller Enterprises		Total (B)	Smaller Enterprises	
		No.	% of A		No.	% of B
Mining . . .	8,205	8,067	98·3	479	176	37·0
Construction .	185,511	185,131	99·8	2,144	1,841	85·9
Manufacturing .	521,305	518,923	99·5	10,193	6,328	62·1
Distribution .	1,749,561	1,737,472	99·3	6,711	5,300	79·0
Finance & Insurance .	23,041	22,836	99·1	} 975	} 197	20·4
Real Estate . .	36,766	36,758	99·99			
Transportation .	44,697	44,191	98·9	} 2,227	} 722	32·3
Elec., Gas, Water .	167	146	87·4			
'Services' . .	646,324	642,137	99·4	3,473	2,634	75·8
Others . . .	226	225	99·9·	—	—	—
Totals .	3,215,402	3,195,885	99·4	26,203	17,198	65·6

NOTES: (i) Smaller enterprises are defined as those which have fewer than 300 personnel, except for distribution, finance and insurance, real estate, and 'services', where the criterion is fewer than 30.

(ii) Unclassifiable employment is included in the public service sector, which does not figure in Table 11.

Source: Based on *Smaller Enterprise White Paper, op. cit.*, Tables 1–1, p. 45, 1–2, p. 46, and 1–7, p. 49.

the moment the general figures may be used to indicate the extent of the difficulty. Distribution absorbs 6·7 million, or 26%, of the industrial labour force which, if we define it as exclusive of those in public service, agriculture, forestry and fisheries, amounts to 26·2 million. Even if we include public service the proportion is still as high as 23%, compared with 14% in the United Kingdom.[6] Concentration in distribution is rapid in countries like Britain and the United States, and although it still has much scope in these countri it is obvious that in Japan great changes are required: 5·3 million— 79%—of the distributive workers are in smaller enterprises and this inefficient use of labour is held to be partly responsible for rapidly rising consumer prices.[7]

Manufacturing industry is also blamed for the recent inflation in consumer goods' prices. It is argued that not only is there a wasteful distribution of resources in the economy as a whole, but more specifically that the structure of Japan's secondary industry is seriously defective compared with other industrial powers. Analyses of, for example, employment distribution, wage differentials, and productivity differentials are deployed to support this view. The contrast between Japan on the one hand, and Britain and the United States on the other, in the distribution of employment in manufacturing comes out clearly in Table 12. In spite of the fact that the Japanese

TABLE 12: *International Comparison of Employment Distribution in Manufacturing According to Scale of Plant*

Scale of Plant (Number of Workers)	Employment (% of Total)		
	Japan (1960)	U.S.A. (1958)	Britain (1951)
1–9	15	4	4(a)
10–49	28	14	11(b)
50–99	11	10	10
100–499	21	30	32
500–999	7	12	13
1000–	17	31	29

(a) 1–10; (b) 11–49.

Sources: Japan in 1960: *Japan Statistical Yearbook 1963*, Table 90, p. 158.

U.S.A. in 1958: Chūshō Kigyō-chō, *Chūshō kigyō kindaika* (Modernisation of Smaller Enterprise), p. 11.

Britain in 1951: P. Sargant Florence, *The Logic of British and American Industry*, 1961, p. 37.

figures are more recent—there has been a steady upward shift of scale in all three countries—54% of the labour force in Japan's manufacturing industry worked in plants of fewer than 100 workers, compared with 28% in the United States, and 25% in Britain. The disparity in the proportions in plants of fewer than 50 workers is even more pronounced: 43% compared with 18% and 15% respectively. In Japan, plants with between 100 and 999 workers absorbed only 28% of the labour force in manufacturing, a much lower proportion than in the United States in 1958 (42%), or in Britain in 1951 (45%).

The contrasts in employment distribution are significant because wage and productivity differentials are much greater in Japan than in other advanced industrial nations. Table 13, which compares wage

TABLE 13: *International Comparison of Wage Differentials*
(*Average wage in plants of 1000 or more workers = 100*)

Scale of Plant (Number of Workers)	Wage Differentials				
	Japan (*1960*)	U.S.A. (*1958*)	France (*1958*)	W. Germany (*1958*)	Britain (*1949*)
1000 or more	100	100	100	100	100
500–999	79	85	91	85	89
300–499	70	79(a)	86(e)	83(g)	86(h)
200–299	64				
100–199	59	77(b)	79		85
50–99	54	74	79	81	84
30–49	50	74(c)	78(f)	—	
20–29	47			—	83(i)
10–19	42	71	78	—	84(j)
4–9	33	67(d)	—	—	—
Average	62	84	—	94	—

(a) 250–499; (b) 100–249; (c) 20–49; (d) 5–9; (e) 200–499; (f) 20–49; (g) 100–499; (h) 200–499; (i) 25–49; (j) 11–24.

Sources: Shinohara Miyohei (ed.), *Sangyō kōzō* (The Structure of Industry), Toyko, 1962, p. 84.
Economic Planning Agency, Japanese Government, *Economic Survey of Japan* (*1962–1963*), Tokyo, n.d. [1963], p. 346.

differentials in a number of countries, shows that it is much more beneficial to the worker in Japan to move into even a *slightly* larger company than it is in, say, the United States or Britain. In these and other countries, a substantial gain is in general obtainable only by moving into the very big plant, and considerable loss is incurred only by dropping into the very small workshop. In Britain the differentials are very small for a wide range in plant-scale: there is only some 3% variation in plants of between 11 and 500 workers. But in Japan the wage differential grows steadily larger through all the grades of plant-scale. Differences in classification make comparisons slightly difficult at some grades, but there can be no doubt that the structure of wages in Japan contains some striking contrasts to the structure in advanced Western countries. There is a bigger differential even in the 500–999 category, and in spite of the classification 300–499 affording a bias in favour of Japan, the figure of 70% contrasts with almost 80% for the United States (200–499), 86% for France (200–499), 83% for West Germany (100–499), and 86% for Britain (200–499). The average Japanese worker in plants of from 50 to 99 workers receives little more than half the average wage of his brothers in the largest plants, while the American worker received three-quarters, and the French, German and British workers about four-fifths. Finally, the differential becomes greater still in Japan in the 10–19 category, while the differentials in the United States, France, and Britain are very little different from those in medium-sized plants (say, 100–500).

The wage differential structure naturally reflects the equally striking structure of productivity differentials in Japan. Table 14 gives the value-added (net-output, in the case of Britain) per worker according to scale in Japan, the United States, and Britain. Again, the wide variations in productivity in Japan are at once noticeable. The older British figures may no longer give a true picture of differentials in Britain—it is important to note that productivity differentials *widened* in the United States and Japan in the 1950s—but even if the gaps increased to the same extent as they did in the United States, the contrast with Japan would be almost as strong. At any rate we may, after noting the great consistency of the British figures, and the fact that even in small plants of 11 to 24 workers productivity was as high as 90% of that in big plants of 1000 or more while in Japan it was less than a third, confine ourselves to a comparison of Japan and the United States. In contrast to America, where the productivity of a worker in a plant of 250–499 employees was only 16% less than that of a worker in the largest plants, in Japan the loss was around 40%. In smaller plants of up to 100 workers in America,

TABLE 14: *International Comparison of Productivity Differentials*
(*Value-added per worker in plants of 1000 or more* = 100)

Scale of Plant (Number of Workers)	Productivity Differentials		
	Japan (1960)	U.S.A. (1958)	Britain (1949)
1000 or more	100	100	100
500–999	80	89	98
300–499	63	84(a)	97(e)
200–299	59		97(e)
100–199	50	79(b)	96
50–99	42	74	94
30–49	37	72(c)	92(f)
20–29	34		92(f)
10–19	29	70	90(g)
4–9	24	70(d)	—

(a) 250–499; (b) 100–249; (c) 20–49; (d) 5–9; (e) 200–499; (f) 25–49; (g) 11–24.

Sources: Same as for Table 13

productivity was still 70 to 74 % of that of the big plants, but in Japan productivity ranged from a mere quarter to a low 42%.

Thus the existence of big and small concerns in industry—a phenomenon found in all industrialised countries, including the most advanced nations—has a special significance for Japan. The reasons for labelling Japanese industrial structure 'dual' or 'two-tier'[8] are not merely that a greater proportion of enterprises are very small and that these absorb a relatively high proportion of the industrial labour force, but that the workers in small enterprises contribute a much smaller amount to the national product, and earn much lower wages, than their counterparts in bigger companies and plants. To this extent, the distribution of manpower, even when we have allowed for the possibility that some of the labour force would not otherwise enter the labour market, is very inefficient.[9] One solution is to effect an upward shift in scale and, as we shall later see in more detail, this has been happening in Japan. Workers must move out of the 10 to 49 employee category, for instance, if it can be assumed that 28 % of the manufacturing labour force in that scale of plant is an unduly high concentration.[10] By international standards this would be of benefit because although productivity differentials are not very great in other leading industrial nations, the gaps are much more significant if unduly high numbers of workers are in the lower categories. But a mere upward shift in scale would not be sufficient in Japan because, even in the 50 to 200 category, productivity is depressingly low on average: only some 40 to 50 % of the largest plants. However, it is, at this stage, useful to consider the changes in industrial scale which occurred during the period of fast growth between 1955 and 1961.

II

The Japanese have been successful in so many of their economic endeavours since 1950 that their self-confessed failure to eradicate dualism is a strange contrast. In every *Economic Survey* and in each of the Economic Plans, high priority has been awarded to measures to remedy the faults of the dual structure, yet the constant necessity to promise solutions in itself reveals the failure of these measures— or, some would insist, the failure to implement the promises. Throughout the 1950s, government objectives included both a high level of heavy industrial output with emphasis on the big, modern plant, and a 'rationalisation' of the many smaller manufacturing concerns, which were urged to merge and modernise their labour structures as well as their technological levels. Promises of financial assistance were made, and exhortations were levelled at the city banks to devote more of their loan resources to the small and medium-sized firms. Since the city banks were fully occupied with satisfying the voracious appetite of the large companies, which were expanding rapidly with the full support of the government, the inconsistencies of the position were clear to everyone. Existing special financial institutions were therefore strengthened and new ones were created to make investment funds available to small business, but it is not surprising that the problem was not solved. To what extent the government's objectives have been totally irreconcilable, and to what extent economic policy has strengthened and not weakened industrial dualism, are questions which probably cannot be fully answered today. But it is possible to measure the changes in industrial structure which occurred in the vital years from 1955 to 1961. In these years, it will be remembered, the Japanese economy underwent many structural changes, changes which included the first significant absolute decline in the agrarian population, a radical drop in the relative importance of the primary sector, both as a source of employment and of national income, a massive switch from light to

TABLE 15: *Number and Scale of Plants in Manufacturing Industry in Japan, 1955–1961.*

Scale of Plant (Number of Workers)	Number of Plants							Increase 1955–1961 (%)
	1955	1956	1957	1958	1959	1960	1961	
1–3	245,593	237,807	248,712	242,647	236,064	248,730	247,360	1
4–9	85,608	84,624	94,265	90,564	87,192	96,943	96,649	13
10–29	74,344	80,074	86,590	87,266	90,093	97,408	101,803	37
30–99	21,086	23,962	26,564	27,048	30,061	33,553	34,541	64
100–299	4,333	4,976	5,517	5,700	6,602	7,588	8,261	91
300–999	1,354	1,491	1,602	1,695	1,930	2,210	2,447	81
1000 or more	376	439	477	452	539	618	689	83
1–299	430,964	431,443	461,648	453,225	450,012	484,222	488,614	13
300 or more	1,730	1,930	2,079	2,147	2,469	2,828	3,136	81
Total	432,694	433,373	463,727	455,372	452,481	487,050	491,750	14

Source: *Smaller Enterprise White Paper, op. cit.,* p. 319.

heavy industry, which involved a great investment effort and concentration of investment funds in steel, machinery, and chemical plant, and, last but not least, a considerable degree of industrial concentration.

The statistics compiled by the Smaller Enterprise Agency for the first White Paper on Small and Medium Enterprise, give support to both the optimists and the pessimists. Superficially, Table 15 shows a dismal failure to reduce the huge number of tiny plants of 1–3 workers in the manufacturing sector: they numbered 245,593 in 1955 and had increased to 247,360 by 1961, after considerable fluctuation in the intervening years. On the other hand, the scale of the economy almost doubled in this period,[11] and there were increases in the numbers of firms in every category. In fact, the statistics could be regarded as encouraging were it not for the enormous size of the small-scale sector at the beginning of the period. The vast number of

TABLE 16: *Distribution of Employment According to Scale in Manufacturing Industry in Japan, 1955–1961* (*000 workers*)

Scale of Plant (No. of Workers)	Number of Workers							
	1955	1956	1957	1958	1959	1960	1961	Increase 1955–1961 (%)
1–3	553	541	563	553	543	568	563	2
4–9	549	548	605	585	569	626	626	14
10–29	1,186	1,290	1,397	1,413	1,464	1,586	1,677	41
30–99	1,027	1,178	1,308	1,340	1,489	1,669	1,743	70
100–299	709	815	901	929	1,072	1,231	1,343	89
300–999	681	751	805	851	970	1,115	1,231	81
1000 or more	805	925	1,024	994	1,188	1,374	1,568	95
1–299	4,024	4,372	4,774	4,820	5,137	5,680	5,952	23
300 or more	1,486	1,676	1,829	1,845	2,158	2,489	2,799	88
Total	5,510	6,048	6,603	6,665	7,295	8,169	8,751	59

Source: *Smaller Enterprise White Paper, op. cit.*, p. 320.

tiny plants employing fewer than 10 workers dominate any statistics which seek to summarise trends in the small-medium categories, and to say that the number of firms falling into those groups increased by only 13% compared with an increase of 81% in the large-scale sector, does not convey the important build-up of medium-sized concerns in these years. Firms with more than 30 workers multiplied much more rapidly than the smaller companies, and the medium-sized concerns of 100–299 personnel multiplied at the fastest rate of all groups: 91% compared with the next highest increase which was 83% in the biggest firms (1000 personnel or more).

The 100–299 group absorbed an appropriate, even a slightly more than proportionate, share of increased employment in manufacturing between 1955 and 1961. Numbers working in these plants rose by 89% (see Table 16), which was a much greater relative increase than in any other small-medium sector, and was exceeded only by the rate of increase in very large plants. So far as the number of plants and the proportion of the labour force are concerned, the trends have, therefore, been quite promising: the crucial group of medium-sized firms expanded rapidly, made relative gains on smaller firms and also on the larger firms of 300–999, and enjoyed an expansion of employment comparable with even the biggest plants. But when we move on to production and investment, the experience of the medium-sized group of firms is somewhat less encouraging. The huge appetite of large-scale industry for investment funds was assuaged, it is true, more by starving the small firms, but the medium and medium-large (100–299 and 300–999) also suffered. Value of shipments, and total value-added figures reflect the continued lag in technological levels, as Tables 17 and 18 show.

Table 17 gives a 172% increase in shipments for medium firms, and this is not only a vastly inferior performance compared with large companies, which absorbed relatively only slightly more labour, but is also inferior to that of medium-large (300–999) companies, which took relatively less labour. The value-added figures of Table 18 also show that big companies were still increasing their proportion of the market in spite of the fast rate at which smaller companies had multiplied and absorbed labour. Big firms quadrupled their value-added figures, while those with labour forces of between 30 and 999 rather less than tripled their net output. In this table, the positions of the three categories 30–99, 100–299, and 300–999, have moved even closer together, and in spite of the variations in percentage increases in number of plants, employment, and shipments, the rate of increase in net output was much the same. Nevertheless, the medium group still showed a slightly larger increase than all other

TABLE 17: *Value of Shipments According to Scale in Manufacturing Industry in Japan, 1955–1961* (¥ *000 million*)

Scale of Plant (No. of Workers)	Value of Shipments							Increase 1955–1961 (%)
	1955	1956	1957	1958	1959	1960	1961	
1–3	208	218	231	231	205	285	319	53
4–9	330	363	412	398	411	500	569	72
10–29	965	1,160	1,325	1,272	1,434	1,743	2,111	119
30–99	1,150	1,442	1,731	1,688	2,012	2,509	3,004	161
100–299	1,141	1,448	1,712	1,705	2,043	2,576	3,107	172
300–999	1,382	1,768	2,094	2,072	2,512	3,206	3,906	183
1000 or more	1,593	2,292	2,953	2,708	3,476	4,760	6,037	279
1–299	3,794	4,631	5,411	5,332	6,105	7,613	9,110	140
300 or more	2,975	4,060	5,047	4,780	5,988	7,966	9,943	234
Total	6,769	8,691	10,458	10,112	12,093	15,579	19,053	181

Source: *Smaller Enterprise White Paper, op. cit.*, p. 321.

TABLE 18: *Value—Added According to Scale in Manufacturing Industry in Japan, 1955–1961 (¥ 000 million).*

Scale of Plant (No. of workers)	Value—Added							
	1955	*1956*	*1957*	*1958*	*1959*	*1960*	*1961*	*Increase 1955–1961 (%)*
4–9	109	116	136	136	146	184	215	97
10–29	292	338	400	415	463	595	737	152
30–99	344	406	517	525	628	817	1,010	194
100–299	341	406	517	509	623	824	1,019	199
300–999	440	529	641	605	806	1,055	1,283	192
1000 or more	574	749	1,020	946	1,315	1,819	2,329	306
4–299	1,086	1,266	1,570	1,585	1,860	2,420	2,981	174
300 or more	1,014	1,278	1,661	1,551	2,121	2,874	3,612	256
Total	2,100	2,544	3,231	3,136	3,981	5,294	6,593	214

Source: *Smaller Enterprise White Paper, op. cit.,* p. 322.

groups, excluding the very big. And certainly this group of firms with 100–299 personnel managed to hold its own slightly better in the investment race.

Table 19 breaks down fixed investment in manufacturing, and, shows that, once again excluding big plants of 1000 or more workers medium-sized firms (100–299) managed to command a relatively greater proportion of investment funds than any other group. However, the medium firms, as a group, did not deepen their capital relative to smaller firms: the ratio of increased employment to increased investment is exactly the same for both the 30–99 and the 100–299 categories. Thus while it is said to be encouraging that there is an upward movement in scale, it is quite obvious that, with the medium group substantially increasing its relative weight in number of plants and employment, technological levels cannot in general have improved very much. There is, of course, great variation in experience within these broad categories, and medium-sized firms in some manufacturing sectors have achieved substantial improvements

TABLE 19: *Fixed Investment According to Scale in Manufacturing Industry in Japan, 1956–1961 (￥000 million)*

Scale of Plant (No. of Workers)	Fixed Investment						
	1956	1957	1958	1959	1960	1961	Increase 1956–1961 (%)
4–9	14	17	15	11	16	21	50
10–29	48	57	51	48	67	96	100
30–99	63	86	76	89	146	193	206
100–299	79	124	95	125	194	283	258
300–999	121	192	162	180	326	415	243
1000 or more	163	284	251	324	512	765	369
4–299	204	284	237	273	423	593	191
300 or more	284	476	413	504	838	1,180	315
Total	488	760	650	777	1,261	1,773	263

Source: *Smaller Enterprise White Paper, op. cit.,* p. 362.

in production processes. One company, which is described above in Chapter 4 and is called Company A, illustrates both tendencies of capital widening and of improved technology, and hope about the future is derived from the movement towards the combination of parts' manufacturers to enable them to specialise, and therefore to introduce mass-production systems. On the other hand, what worries many people is the backwardness of so many other firms, a backwardness which is reflected in the averages of our tables.

It is useful to look at these changes between 1955 and 1961 to see how they affected the structure of manufacturing. In Table 20 the previous tables are summarised and put in the perspective of the industry as a whole. Medium firms grew relative to other groups of small-medium businesses, and there was an encouraging upward shift in scale. Tiny plants of fewer than 10 workers were markedly less preponderant in number in 1961, and the 1–3 category declined in relative importance from 57% to 50%. But analysts insist that the upward shift in scale is less favourable than it seems because the performance of small and medium-scale plants has lagged so far behind that of large firms that in spite of the relative increase in

TABLE 20: *Changes in the Structure of Manufacturing Industry in Japan, 1955–1961 (%)*

Scale of Plant (No. of Workers)	No. of Plants		Total Employment		Total Shipments		Total Value-Added		Total Fixed Investment	
	1955	1961	1955	1961	1955	1961	1955	1961	1956	1961
1–3	56·75	50·30	10	7	3	2	n.a.	n.a.	n.a.	n.a.
4–9	19·78	19·45	10	7	5	3	6	3	2·9	1·2
10–29	17·17	20·70	21	19	9	11	14	12	9·8	5·4
30–99	4·88	7·02	19	20	18	16	16	15	12·9	10·9
100–299	1·00	1·68	13	15	18	16	16	15	16·3	15·9
300–999	0·31	0·50	12	14	22	20	21	20	24·8	23·4
1000 or more	0·09	0·14	15	18	25	32	27	35	33·3	43·2
1–299	99·60	99·36	73	68	56	48	52*	45*	41·9*	33·4*
300 or more	0·40	0·64	27	32	44	52	48	55	58·1	66·6
Total	100·00	100·00	100	100	100	100	100	100	100·00	100·00

* Plants with 4–299 workers.

Source: *Smaller Enterprise White Paper, op. cit.,* pp. 319, 320, 321, 332 and 362.

F

number of, and employment in, small-medium businesses of 30 to 299 workers, the value which they added actually fell from 16% to 15% of the total. In fact, this is also true for the medium-large plants of 300–999 workers: in spite of an increased share of employment (12% to 14%), their share of shipments fell from 22% to 20% and their share of value-added fell from 21% to 20%.

The complaint that big business is becoming as powerful as it was before the Second World War is based not only on the familiar discrepancies between the small-medium firms and the giants, but also on the widening gap between the medium-large (300–999) and the very large. Failure to achieve efficient methods of production is attributed to the failure of *all* categories of plants of less than 1000 workers to maintain their share of investment funds at a time when some of the categories were increasing their share of total employment. Official agencies could hardly avoid admitting their bias towards heavy large-scale industry, when the statistics revealed that this sector had increased its share of total fixed investment from

TABLE 21: *Value—Added per Worker According to Scale in Manufacturing Industry in Japan, 1955–1961 (¥ 000).*

Scale of Plant (No. of Workers)	Value—Added per Worker							
	1955	1956	1957	1958	1959	1960	1961	Increase 1955–1961 (%)
4–9	199	212	225	232	257	294	343	72
10–29	246	262	286	294	316	375	439	78
30–99	335	345	395	392	422	490	579	73
100–299	481	498	574	548	581	670	759	58
300–999	646	704	796	711	831	946	1,042	61
1000 or more	713	810	996	952	1,107	1,324	1,485	108
4–299	313	330	373	371	405	473	553	77
300 or more	682	763	908	841	983	1,155	1,290	89
Average	424	462	535	513	590	696	805	90

Source: *Smaller Enterprise White Paper, op. cit.,* p. 323.

one-third to over two-fifths. In the same period, even the rapidly expanding medium sized sector (100–299) commanded only 15·9% of investment in 1961, as against 16·3% in 1955. Larger firms of up to 1000 workers suffered an even greater relative decline: from 24·8% to 23·4%.

Productivity increases have, in general, been very high in Japanese manufacturing, and the quite substantial advances made in productivity in the plants falling into the 4 to 99 categories (see Table 21 on the opposite page) support Shinohara's argument that the depreciated value of second-hand equipment, bought by the small companies from the big companies, understates its value as a productive asset.[12] Capital-output ratios may well have been much lower in the smaller firms, and their failure to command the same share of fixed investment funds may not, therefore, be of quite so much significance as the figures in Table 20 suggested. Nevertheless, as Table 21 shows, productivity advanced considerably more slowly in plants of less than 1000, and, more particularly, in plants of 100 to 299 workers, than in the big plants of over 1000 workers. Once again, it is necessary to emphasise that there will have been great variations in experience within these categories, but the overall lag in productivity was, when the rapid rise in wages in small-medium businesses is taken into account, becoming more and more serious as a general problem during the later 1950s.

Big plants of more than 1000 workers more than doubled productivity between 1955 and 1961, while those of fewer than 1000 did not achieve an increase of more than three-fifths to three-quarters. In the same period, according to figures given in Table 22, wages increased by only 45% in the big plants compared with increases of from 52% to 72% in the categories of up to 299 workers. Medium-large plants (300–999) kept down wage increases even more effectively than the largest plants. The narrowing of wage differentials in plants of up to 299 workers (see Table 23 on p. 65) was regarded with mixed feelings in Japan: the relative improvement was welcomed as an erosion of the dualism which is widely regarded as one of Japan's black spots, but it was attributed to the end of abundant labour supplies rather than to the improved ability of small entrepreneurs to pay higher wages. This is a difficult matter to judge. In no category was the rate of wage increase faster than the rate of productivity increase. For instance, wages in plants of 100–299 workers went up by 52% between 1955 and 1961, compared with an improvement in productivity of 58%. But this, from the employers' point of view, was a poor showing compared with the big firms' increased productivity of 108%, and wage increases of only 45%.

TABLE 22: *Wage per Worker According to Scale in
Manufacturing Industry in Japan, 1955–1961 (¥ 000)*

Scale of Plant (No. of workers)	Annual Wage per Worker							
	1955	1956	1957	1958	1959	1960	1961	Increas₂ 1955–1961 (%)
4–9	87	91	96	102	108	119	144	66
10–29	110	116	125	131	139	157	189	72
30–99	133	140	152	158	168	187	223	68
100–299	165	172	187	190	197	217	250	52
300–999	209	218	234	240	245	268	299	43
1000 or more	270	295	323	336	334	359	392	45
4–299	125	132	143	149	158	177	210	68
300 or more	242	260	284	291	294	318	351	45
Average	160	171	185	192	201	223	258	61

Source: *Smaller Enterprise White Paper, op. cit.*, p. 324.

Margins in small businesses, even with low wages and abundant labour, have always been considered to be too low to make much self-financing possible, and it could be that even the small improvement in differentials came too quickly. Yet small it certainly was: it will be seen from Table 23 that, taking wages in plants of more than 1000 workers as the base, the wage in small plants of fewer than 100 workers increased faster relative to the wage in big plants than did the wage in the intermediate categories, but the increase was by no means impressive. Furthermore, not only was the improvement in medium-sized businesses very small—a narrowing of the differential from 61% to 64%—but the differential in medium-large companies (300–999) actually widened, from 77% to 76%.

When we look at the productivity differentials given in Table 23, the problems of small-medium business in this period are underlined. Wage differentials narrowed, but productivity differentials grew rapidly, and, moreover, the gap widened most of all for the medium and medium-large groups. In 1961 the net output of a worker in the average medium-scale plant (100-299) was only 51% of the net output of the employee of the big plant, whereas in 1955 it had been 67%. The productivity record in medium-large (300-999) was just as bad: a widening differential from 91% to 70% represents a relative deterioration which was almost exactly the same as that for medium-scale companies. There are always gaps between best and worst practice in any economy, but the correlation with *scale* seems to be much closer in Japan, and the persistence, indeed the enhancing, of these differentials was regarded as one of Japan's most serious industrial problems. Wages rose faster, but relative productivity deteriorated sharply, in small-medium plants.

TABLE 23: *Productivity and Wage Differentials in Manufacturing Industry in Japan, 1955–1961*
(Plants with 1000 or more workers = 100)

Scale of Plant (No. of Workers)	Value—Added per Worker		Annual Wage per Worker	
	1955	1961	1955	1961
4–9	28	23	32	37
10–29	34	30	41	48
30–99	47	39	49	57
100–299	67	51	61	64
300–999	91	70	77	76
1000 or more	100	100	100	100

Source: *Smaller Enterprise White Paper, op. cit.*, pp. 323 and 324.

It is sometimes misleading to speak of a 'labour shortage' in Japan, although such references are increasingly common, but the mounting difficulty in obtaining *young* workers has recently produced some unusual effects. The 1964 spring wage offensive[13] by the unions dealt a further blow to small and medium-scale businesses at a time when restrictive monetary policies were throwing them into crisis: unions adopted a most unsympathetic attitude towards the employers' difficulties because according to the Tokyo Metropolitan Labour Bureau (*Tōkyō-to Rōdōkyoku*) there was practically no difference in the size of wage demands being made by unions in small-medium enterprises, and those being made in the big companies.[14] This came when a post-war record in bankruptcy statistics for small-medium businesses had already been established in February, and yet another record was clearly on the way in March, 1964. We shall now go on to describe this episode in the history of economic policy and industrial dualism in Japan.

III

The promises made during the General Election campaign in the autumn of 1963 that positive measures to solve the problems caused by dualism would be taken by the government, were almost immediately followed, after the government had been returned to power, by monetary policies which, it seemed to many at the time, would in fact damage the smaller enterprises even more. The large international payments deficits at the end of 1963, the continued rapid growth of industrial production, and the imminence of trade liberalisation measures booked for the spring of 1964, induced the government to launch a credit squeeze from the middle of December 1963. The tight money policy strengthened from an increase in reserve deposit ratios on December 16th, to a rise in the Bank Rate in March 1964. There was a simultaneous upsurge of bankruptcies of small and medium-sized concerns, which provoked sharp criticism of government policies and worried reactions in the ruling Liberal-Democratic Party (*Jimintō*), whose Small Enterprise Committee strongly urged that help be given to small businesses.

The explanations of the bankruptcies were varied. Some economists continued to emphasise dualism as both the ultimate and the immediate cause. Others, while acknowledging the underlying weaknesses produced by the dual industrial structure, stressed bad management and wrong forecasting as the reasons for the current crisis.[15] The Finance Ministry issued a statement which was headlined in the *Asahi Shimbun: Hiki-shime ga genin de nai*—'Tight money is not the cause'.[16] The statement was based on reports from the Ministry's regional finance bureaux, and it insisted that the majority of bankruptcies was caused by (*a*) over-investment in equipment, and (*b*) mistaken estimates of demand; (*c*) the cessation of assistance to small firms by contracting companies; and (*d*) chain reactions resulting from individual bankruptcies. The warm winter had also had, it was said, an effect on certain branches of manufacturing such as winter clothing and heating appliances. The action of the contracting companies was particularly emphasised, and this was attributed not to tight money but to a general reorganisation which was being undertaken in preparation for the progressive liberalisation of the economy: weak firms were being eliminated in order to rationalise and strengthen commercial organisation. In the Ministry's view, therefore, it was not necessary to take any special supplementary financial measures for small and medium enterprise.[17]

A survey made at the same time by the Tokyo Commercial and Industrial Agency (*Tōkyō Shōkō Kōshin-sho*) did acknowledge that the credit squeeze might be a factor in some failures, but largely agreed with the Ministry's view that it was not the principal cause. It confirmed the Ministry's analysis, with rather more emphasis on internal managerial and structural deficiencies. The survey revealed that the February figures of bankruptcies and unliquidated liabilities were a post-war record. Bankruptcies of firms with debts of ¥10 millions or more had numbered 194 in December 1963, 198 in January 1964, and had jumped to 238 in February. Total liabilities were ¥23,900 millions, ¥28,200 millions, and ¥35,100 millions respectively[18].

The importance of the role of 'parent' companies and other contracting companies was stressed more and more as the months went by. Thus in April it was said that examples of these companies withdrawing support were increasing, with a consequent increase in the instability of small and medium businesses. Further statistics from the Tokyo Commercial and Industrial Agency showed that another post-war record of bankruptcies had been established in March, when there were 275 failures with a new record of indebtedness of ¥35,500 million. A disturbing feature was the much higher proportion of failures in chemical and metallurgical concerns, in contrast to earlier in the year when textile and heating-appliance manufacturers had predominated in the bankruptcy statistics, because failures in chemical and metallurgical industries could hardly be attributed, even in part, to the mild winter. Furthermore, there had been a steady increase in failures in rather larger business: bankruptcies of companies with debts of ¥100 million or more had numbered twenty-nine in September 1963, fifty-seven in November 1963, fifty-seven in January 1964, and eighty-three in March 1964. These failures accounted for four-fifths of total liabilities. A sharp deterioration in the terms imposed upon sub-contractors was now thought to be a primary cause: lower cash proportions, extension of bills, and cuts in unit prices in such subcontracting spheres as machinery and automobile parts were prevalent. There could be no doubt of the influence—both direct and indirect—of the credit squeeze in contributing to the increase in bankruptcies.[19]

In fact, whenever measures to help small business were announced, they were almost always accompanied by references to the tight-money policy, and there was a flood of such measures in this period. On 16 December 1963—on the same day that reserve deposit ratios were raised—the Finance Ministry announced that Small Business Finance Corporation (*Chūshō Kigyō Kinyū Kōko*) debentures amounting to some ¥10,000 million would be issued under a government guarantee to augment the funds available for loan to smaller businesses.[20] Shortly after this it was forecast that advances from the various special financial institutions for small and medium enterprise would be increased by 17% in the 1964–1965 financial year. Funds from the Treasury Loan and Investment Account to these institutions were also to be increased substantially over the 1963–1964 levels: from ¥66,800 million to ¥83,300 million for the Small Business Finance Corporation, from ¥56,500 million to ¥69,400 million for the People's Finance Corporation (*Kokumin Kinyū Kōko*), and from ¥5,000 million to ¥9,000 million for the Central Cooperative Bank for Commerce and Industry (*Shōkō Kumiai Chūō Kinko*).[21]

On 21 January 1964, the Prime Minister reiterated the government's determination to modernise small and medium-scale businesses, which would be helped to raise their technological levels through the installation of new machinery, and also helped to improve their managerial techniques. Measures to be adopted would include low interest loans for modern equipment, and more assistance from public funds (grants would be increased to ¥16,565 million in the 1964–1965 budget). In these ways the necessary funds to increase both the quantity and quality of production would be forthcoming.[22]

But from January right through 1964, the major concern shifted from investment funds to the desperate shortage of working capital for smaller businesses. The experience of one of the companies described in the next chapter was not unique: unfavourable terms from contracting companies were reinforced by a cessation of bank accommodation.[23] Exhortations to the city banks to be lenient with small businesses appear to have met with so little response that on 19 March 1964 the Prime Minister announced that a ban on 'forced deposits' in commercial banks was forthwith introduced. These deposits were the proportion of bank advances and even of proceeds from bills discounted by the banks, which the borrower was forced to leave in his account, a practice which considerably raised the effective interest burden. The ban was prompted by the imminent rise in the interest rates charged on loans to 'financially weak small and medium enterprises',[24] resulting from the increase in the Bank Rate on March 18th.

The ban was only one of the measures which followed hot on the heels of the increased Bank Rate. The Tax Administration Bureau immediately decided on broad measures of assistance for small companies suffering from the tight money policy. All local Tax Administration Bureaux were instructed to allow, under certain circumstances, up to two years for tax payments, to expedite refunds of any excess tax charges and, in appropriate cases, to allow the payment of taxes by instalments.[25] Even purely commercial undertakings like Tokyo Electric Power (*Tōkyō Denryoku*) joined in the rescue operation: the Corporation announced on 19 March that smaller companies in financial difficulties from the credit squeeze would be allowed to pay electricity bills on the same instalment terms accorded to large consumers. 'Minimal' interest rates would be charged on delayed payments.[26]

During March, as it became clear that yet another bankruptcy record would be established, the Smaller Enterprise Agency urged many measures, ranging from a systematisation of joint consultation between the various ministries concerned with the smaller enterprise problem, to special consideration for these businesses when allocating contracts.[27] Both national and prefectural government agencies and departments were urged to cooperate to increase the orders going to small concerns. The procedure for settling contracts and specification requirements could, it was suggested, be relaxed for their benefit. Yet, as the Agency itself stated, during 1963–1964 small and medium businesses had in fact already secured 84% of the total *number* of contracts awarded,[28] and the scope for increasing this percentage must surely be very limited. The 84% represented only 38% of the total *value* of the contracts, but in general big contracts must go to big companies. Cooperation between small companies might increase the scope for dealing with larger contracts, but the Agency's suggestion that even the big contracts, if divided into separate operations, would provide work for more of the smaller concerns could well have an adverse affect on efficiency if it were put into practice.

By the end of March 1964 more firms had failed than in any other month since the Second World War, yet it was becoming apparent that the worst was still to come. At the beginning of April there was general agreement that the peak of the crisis for small firms would be reached sometime between April and June, after which, it was hoped, there would be relaxation of the tight money policy. To help tide over this period the three special finance institutions catering for smaller concerns planned to increase their advances by about 30% over the corresponding quarter of 1963, but they all emphasised the grave dilemma facing their customers: investment in modernisation was essential, but the demand for investment funds was down compared with 1963. The immediate need was for working capital because of the action of contracting companies and because of the credit squeeze, but a major cause of financial instability was over-borrowing. Since it was inevitable that many of the increased advances would merely increase the debt burden without improving the performance of the companies, the new deal for small business was turning sour. The People's Finance Corporation reported that fifty-five of their customers had gone bankrupt between October 1963 and February 1964. The Corporation stressed bad management and over-borrowing, but also referred to the price-cuts and unfavourable payment conditions imposed on the small companies by their big customers. More failures could be expected between April and June.[29] On 30 April, the Tokyo Commercial and Industrial Agency published the tally for April: yet another record of 332 bankruptcies (there had been 275 in March, itself a record figure), with liabilities standing at a new high of ¥36,395 million.[30]

The next chapter will, it is hoped, illustrate some of the problems which the smaller companies face, both in crises such as the one described above, and in their relationships with other firms in the complicated network of subcontracting, which is so prominent a characteristic of the structure of Japanese industry.

REFERENCES

1 The former Director-General of the Economic Planning Agency, Kenichi Miyazawa. Cf. *Nihon Keizai Shimbun*, 12 October, 1963.

2 The former Minister for International Trade and Industry, Hajime Fukuda, in his foreword to the first White Paper on Small-Medium Enterprise: Chūshō Kigyō-chō (Smaller Enterprise Agency), *Chushō kigyō hakusho Shōwa 38 nendo* (White Paper on Small-Medium Enterprise for 1963–1964), Tokyo, 1964; hereafter cited as Smaller Enterprise White Paper.

3 Yamanaka Tokutarō (ed.), *Keizai seichō to chūshō kigyō*, Tokyo, 1963, pp. 3–11.

4 Sometimes it is possible to distinguish between the number of enterprises and the number of plants in each category of scale, but it is often impossible, and Japanese statisticians do not fail to point out the defects in their statistics.

If anything, however, these seem to *under*state the extent of differences in productivity and other indicators as between large and small businesses. See, for example, p. 1 of the Explanatory Notes (*hanrei*) of the Smaller Enterprise White Paper cited above in footnote 2.

5 The difference in classification does not affect the percentages very much. In fact, as we shall see, it is precisely in the middle range that Japan's weakness lies. The American figures are from the Department of Commerce, *Factory Statistics for 1958*, quoted in Chūshō Kigyō-chō, *Chūshō kigyō kindaika no jitsumu* (The Administration of The Modernisation of Small-Medium Enterprise, Tokyo, 1964, p. 11.

6 The United Kingdom figure for 1961 is calculated from National Economic Development Council, *op. cit.*, Table 6, p. 23.

7 The pitfalls in the concept of under-employment are many, but it is at least likely that a large number of family workers, as well as of employees, in distribution is a potential labour force for other sectors. Many might well move on if the masters transferred to other occupations.

8 Since the links between large and small businesses are very close, the more literal translation of *nijū kōzō* is, for some purposes, more enlightening.

9 That is, inefficient in an economy where there are complaints about a growing shortage of labour. The past role of the dual structure in absorbing large numbers of workers who might otherwise have swelled the ranks of the unemployed or underemployed has to be viewed in a different context.

10 The corresponding figure in the United States was 14%: see above, Table 12, p. 50.

11 Cf. Keizai Kikaku-chō (Economic Planning Agency), *Kokumin shotoku hakusho Shōwa 37 nendo* (National Income White Paper for 1962–63), Tokyo, 1964, p. 160. Real gross national product increased from ¥8,235,500 million in 1955, to ¥15,221,500 in 1961.

12 Miyohei Shinohara, *Growth and Cycles in the Japanese Economy*, pp. 23–25. For more detail on this point, see below, Ch. 4, p. 76.

13 These offensives are held annually.

14 *Asahi Shimbun*, 29 March, 1964.

15 See the analysis of academic comment in *Asahi Shimbun*, 28 February, 1964.

16 *Ibid.*, 6 March, 1964.

17 *Nihon Keizai Shimbun*, 6 March, 1964.

18 *Ibid., loc. cit.*

19 *Ibid.*, 12 April, 1964.

20 *Ibid.*, 17 December, 1963 (evening edition).

21 *Ibid.*, 30 December, 1963. Interest rates charged by the first two corporations on advances would not be increased, while the Cooperative Bank's rates would be lowered.

22 *Nihon Keizai Shimbun*, 21 January, 1964 (evening edition).

23 See below, Ch. 4, pp. 82–83.

24 *Japan Times*, 20 March, 1964.

25 *Asahi Shimbun*, 19 March, 1964.

26 *Ibid.*, 20 March, 1964.

27 *Ibid.*, 29 March, 1964.

28 *Ibid.*, 11 March, 1964.

29 *Nihon Keizai Shimbun*, 3 April, 1964.

30 *Asahi Shimbun*, 1 May, 1964.

CHAPTER 4

Industrial Dualism
and the
Subcontracting System

I

A crucial element in the organisation of Japanese industry is one which, while not unique in comparison with other advanced industrial nations, is nevertheless sufficiently different in character to warrant special emphasis. Subcontracting, in Japan, is both a cause and a result of the special place Japanese industry occupies in statistics of wage and productivity differentials, and in scale of plant and employment distribution. There is no simple explanation of the survival of vast numbers of smaller and medium companies: in Chapter 1 we traced some of the most important factors which determined the development of industrial dualism. The continued existence of small scale industry catering for traditional consumption habits obviously requires explanations which are different in kind from the reasons which led to dualism within the 'modern' sector. Some of the factors relevant to the discussion of the modern sector, factors such as the dual labour market, and the composition of fixed assets in small firms, help to explain not only the continued ability of such firms to compete with bigger companies in the production of similar products, but also the ability of some of the categories of small and medium companies to expand at a rate which is, or has been until recently, quite comparable with the rate of expansion of big concerns. In addition, however, there are vast numbers of companies which do not rely on their ability to compete with larger companies. These are the dependent companies, companies which have either direct subcontracting relationships with big firms or indirect links via companies which are sometimes only slightly above them in scale of operations. It is this type of company which has been, for so many years, the subject of acrimonious debate, and has appeared to justify the accusations of exploitation and of 'precapitalistic' or 'feudalistic' oppression.

72

The Japanese automobile industry, for example, contains structural features which are both the hope and the despair of analysts of Japanese industrial organisation. There are medium-scale firms which invest in modernisation and are helping to create an industry which is conforming more closely to the desired picture of 'western' industrialisation; and at the same time there are small units which display all the undesirable characteristics of a 'pre-capitalist' backward economy. If there is one industry which epitomises modern mass production, it is the automobile industry, yet in Japan its structure helps to explain the charge, levelled by many Japanese, that their economy combines the ultra-modern with the ultra-backward in organisation even within a single industry.

Towering over the hundreds of smaller firms are huge modern automobile assembly plants like those of Isuzu at Fujisawa or Nissan at Oppama. Although the Japanese automobile industry does not yet produce passenger-cars on anything like the American or Western European scale, and although there are criticisms that there are too many assembly firms, it is still true—as in other countries—that the big Japanese automobile producers are few in number, with life becoming increasingly difficult for those not in the top flight of production statistics. Toyota and Nissan are the giants of the passenger-car industry,[1] while Isuzu is making great efforts to add a larger car-output to its substantial share of heavy commercial vehicle production. Output by these and other companies, such as Hino Motors and Prince Motors, has increased rapidly since 1957, and Japan has improved its world position from seventh to fifth place (all vehicles), from ninth to seventh (passenger cars), and fifth to second (commercial vehicles).[2] Second only to the United States in the output of trucks and buses, Japan produces 75% more units in this sector than does Britain, which lies third.

This extremely rapid growth—much higher than that of any other prominent automobile-producing country, with the single exception of Brazil[3]—has produced an industry which is dominated by a small number of fiercely competing companies, each of which is pouring investment into beautifully equipped, extensively laid-out plants. These companies certainly do present a vivid contrast to many of the medium, small, and tiny enterprises which supply them with parts and accessories, and which are often absolutely dependent upon one great assembler. But the complicated structure of the industry embraces very diverse relationships, relationships which will be illustrated by the following account, and which cannot be summed up by the charge that the modern plant is concerned only to exploit the smaller businesses which depend on it.

II

The Ōmori district of Tokyo is well-known for its large numbers of small and medium-sized businesses, many of which are linked either directly or indirectly with great engineering companies. One such medium-scale firm, which we shall call Company A, was, in March 1964, both a subcontractor to Isuzu Motors, and a 'parent' company for yet smaller subcontractors.[4] Its founder had been a fisherman (like his father) until the age of 24, when he became a *honkō* or permanent employee in the automobile department of the Ishikawajima Shipbuilding Company.[5] After ten years with Ishikawajima, during which time he became a foreman, he gave up his regular employment to manage a sub-contracting group in the same motor-works. This meant that he had no factory or equipment of his own, but employed a small number of workers on his own account. He himself, like his workers, now had no permanent status within the Ishikawajima organisation, whose conditions of employment applied only to its regular workers. This system is still widespread today.

In 1939, after some three years in this capacity of internal sub-contracting, he was able to establish his own workshop, with three employees. No other Ishikawajima worker went with him, and he received no financial assistance from the Company at this time. His capital of ¥49,000[6] was derived from his and his father's savings, and there was initially no borrowed capital. The one thing that was obtained from Ishikawajima was a verbal agreement that he would be provided with contracts. This was a good time for gaining a foothold in the automobile-parts manufacturing industry: it was not difficult to expand production with the economy switching over to a wartime basis between 1939 and 1941, when war with America finally broke out. In the same period, the total workforce rose from four to twenty, and the business was made into a limited liability company with a share capital of ¥196,000, of which 25% (the original ¥49,000) was paid-up.

The company was expanded gradually during the 1950s, and it shared in the great boom of 1959–1961 when the Japanese automobile industry was making rapid progress. Between 1955 and 1961 the labour force doubled, from 60 to 120, but it was in the boom period that the company moved firmly into the ranks of the medium-sized group of enterprises, with a 50% increase in the labour force in 1960 and 1961. At the same time a fixed investment programme was initiated which completely transformed the company. Again, it shared in the general pattern of Japanese industrial expansion, relying very heavily on borrowed money. In a 'normal' year, it was said, roughly ¥10 million would be invested, and this would be financed to the extent of 80% from the banks, 10% from depreciation allowances, and 10% from reserves. The nature of the impulse given by the boom of 1959–1961 is conveyed by the figure of ¥93 million raised in 1960 and 1961. From the usual level of some ¥8 million of bank loans, borrowings jumped to ¥25 million in 1960, and ¥60 million in 1961. In March 1964 outstanding debts to banks totalled about ¥95 million.

These loans came principally from the special financial institutions which have been evolved in Japan to provide finance for the smaller enterprises. The *Nippon Sōgo Ginkō* (The Mutual Loans and Savings Bank of Japan) was the most important source of investment funds, and it was also the channel for credit provided by the *Chūshō Kigyō Kinyū Kōko* (Small Business Finance Corporation). These banks provided over 70% of the funds and the remainder came from, first of all, the local Jōnan credit association (*Jōnan Shinyō Kinko*), and, lastly, from two of the city banks—the Mitsubishi and Yokohama Banks. The special institutions were designed to fill the gap left by the city banks' concentration on large-scale business.

Although Company A was able to take advantage of these special facilities, it is important to note that its general manager insisted that without the backing of Isuzu Motors these loans would not have been forthcoming. The backing amounted to more than a confirmation that the company was expanding largely on the basis of contracts from Isuzu. Isuzu actually guaranteed one-third of the loans, and it does seem that even in this case of an expanding, healthy company, subordination remains strong, even necessary. Furthermore, the conditions of borrowing were not particularly easy: the average rate of interest on the loans, all of which were for five year periods, was about 9%, the annual interest burden was ¥8·2 million, and annual repayments amounted to ¥20 million. In 1963 net profit was ¥11·6 million.

There had also been some expansion of the share capital. The original stock had been held by the founder, who was still the company's president. In 1959 this amounted to ¥2 million, but in 1960 and 1961 was quintupled to ¥10 million. There were no outside shareholders, but there had been sales of the new stock to employees. In March 1964 the president held 50%, his son, who was general manager, held 20%, and employees owned 30%. The increase of ¥8 million in share capital was large compared with 1959, but it was dwarfed by the ¥85 million of borrowed capital in the same years.

Dependence on the 'parent' company extended beyond contracts and financial backing. The funds were raised to renovate the existing factory buildings and to reorganise their layout, to build a third workshop in 1961, and to instal new machinery. New machines were well in evidence, but it is interesting to note that in spite of the heavy borrowing, A was still dependent on Isuzu for the loan of some of the more expensive machines. About ¥25 million of machinery was on hire at a monthly rent of 2% of the retail price. The machines could be bought after a few years at their depreciated value. Since the Japanese tax system has made generous provision for accelerated depreciation, this system presumably has advantages for both companies: it ensures to the assembler an increased supply of better parts and accessories; it enables him to exercise some control over the kind of machines used in the smaller company; it makes technical assistance to the smaller company easier and more effective; and it helps the subcontractor to rationalise his layout and move towards mass-production as his assembler grows in size. Miyohei Shinohara has pointed out that an important element in the beneficial effects of the dual industrial structure on the rate of economic growth, in Japan at least, has been the absorption into the small-scale sector of machines discarded by the big firms. The proportion of second-hand fixed assets gets steadily bigger as the size of the manufacturing business decreases, and was as high as a third to one half in firms of between four and fifty employees in 1954.[7] It may always be difficult for small and medium-sized businesses to get finance, but in Japan a mitigating factor has been the opportunity to buy second-hand machines, and this has enabled small and medium firms to expand with the economy and with big business.[8] It is more than probable that the close relationship between assemblers and subcontractors has been of immense importance in dictating technological patterns in both big and small companies. The proportions of second-hand assets mentioned above have declined since the early 1950s, and if Company A is any guide, a more important factor in the 1960s is the help given in installing new machines. Even where the sale and purchase of second-hand equipment remains important, the technological level may still be much higher in the smaller firms than it used to be. This is because the rate of investment in new equipment has been so enormous in Japan since the early 1950s. The country has a higher proportion of new machines than does Britain, for example, and the tax incentives—implicit in the accelerated depreciation scheme—to instal new machinery, and therefore to dispose of used, but still comparatively new, equipment to dependent subcontractors must have been very important. This is further reinforced by the evident desire of the big assembler to promote the development of larger and more efficient subcontractors.

The peculiarities and problems of the Japanese labour market are illustrated by the composition of Company A's working force. It is often suggested that there are two broad divisions of the labour market: the market for the big enterprise and the market for the smaller firms. Many of the characteristics which are emphasised in discussion of industrial employment in Japan belong only to the system that operates in big companies, and even here too little attention is sometimes paid to the prevalence of temporary labour and of subcontract labour, both inside and outside the big plant. For instance, the belief that the Japanese worker is the subject of paternalistic care, that he is typically a life-long employee of the same firm, and that he benefits from a company-created miniature welfare-state, is true only of the workers in big enterprise, and of those who form that part of the big company's labour force which is classified as *honkō*—permanent employees. This proportion varies with the state of business, although the absolute number of permanent workers may be surprisingly constant in some industrial sectors.[9] Variations in total labour force are often determined solely by variations in the numbers of temporary (*rinjikō*) and subcontract (*shagaikō*) labour. The employment conditions of the last two groups are completely separate from those of the regular workers. To this extent, the contrast between the labour markets for the big, and for the small companies is blurred, although it remains true that the former typically attract mainly high-school and university graduates, while the latter often draw upon the reservoir of older, more experienced workers. There is little or no flow of labour from the small firm to the big (except for temporary or subcontract employment), but there is a considerable flow from big to small.

Company A, a medium-scale firm, had a total labour force of 151 in March, 1964. There was no division into *honkō*, *rinjikō*, and *shagaikō*—all were '*honkō*', but there was a strong implication that these divisions had little meaning for this type of firm. In theory, the system of *nenkō-joretsu*—payment of wages according to length of service—which is widely practised in big companies, did operate, but since the average length of service was only three to four years, in practice the system had little relevance. Labour turnover was thus extremely high:

TABLE 24: *Labour Turnover in Company A, 1961–1963*

	Pay-roll	Turnover	Turnover %
1961	120	31	26
1962	140	59	42
1963	151	42	28

G

The average age of employees was about 28 years and there were no examples of retirement pay (*taishokkin*), although the company had been in existence for twenty-five years. There had been cases of workers aged fifty-five and over who had retired, but these were all ineligible for retirement pay because they had joined the company after retiring from a bigger firm. All the older workers currently employed were in the same position, and with such a high turnover it was extremely unlikely that the company would be faced with expenditure on retirement pay unless and until it expanded into a major concern.

The high turnover was not a result of dismissals: in this respect the saying that in Japan no one gets sacked seems of general application. In 1961 only one of the thirty-one who left the firm was dismissed, and this case was, apparently, the nearest approach to dismissal for an unsatisfactory work record in the company's history. The man concerned had told a factory inspector that he was too busy to observe factory regulations. Of the 101 employees who left in 1962 and 1963, only four were dismissed (all in 1963), and the reason here was cited as 'immorality', which turned out to be petty-thieving. The most important reason for the high turnover lay in the nature of the work and the kind of worker it attracted. Much of the work involved repetitive, semi-skilled operations, and the operatives were the type who would constantly be on the lookout for such jobs as lorry- or taxi-driving. Another factor was the contrast between the work performed in Company A and the much lighter, cleaner work in the rapidly expanding electrical goods industry, which was attracting workers every year.

Even so, and in spite of the current severe shortage of young people in the Japanese labour market—and such a shortage of young workers contrasts very sharply with the problem of juvenile unemployment in the United States and also in Britain at times—a large number of the workers were high-school graduates, although two-thirds of these were naturally concentrated in clerical, supervisory, and technical capacities.[10] As Table 25 shows, 22% of the labour force had a high-school or university education, and these had been attracted, in a market in which it was estimated early in 1964 that there were between three and four jobs available for every high school graduate, only by successive and substantial increases in hiring wages. In March 1964, hiring wages had reached ¥12,000 per month for middle-school graduates, ¥15,000 for high-school graduates, and ¥18,000 for university graduates. The average basic wage of non-supervisory and non-technical personnel was ¥18,000 per month, which was increased to rather more than ¥20,000 by

TABLE 25: *Employment in Company A, December, 1963*

(i) *Employment Structure*

	Clerical, Supervisory and Technical	Production	Totals
Male . .	13	121	134
Female . .	10	6	16
Totals . .	23	127	150

(ii) *Educational Qualifications*

	University Graduates	High School Graduates	Middle School Graduates
Clerical, Supervisory and Technical .	4	19	—
Production . ,	—	10	117

overtime pay. In addition—as is general—biannual bonuses were paid which, in 1963, amounted to one-and-a-half months' pay in July and one-and-three-quarter months' pay in December. So the average monthly income would have been roughly ¥25,000 per month. Although this average includes the older workers, who might be expected to earn more, it was in practice quite close to the average paid to workers in their late teens and very early twenties. The gap between the wages of the worker in his thirties and those of the new recruit was narrowing steadily. Generally speaking, the company had in recent years tried to limit the annual increment to about ¥1000 per month, but the growing shortage of young labour had necessitated increases in the wages of workers already on the pay-roll as the hiring wage had risen. But this necessity disappears, apparently, around the age of twenty-two to twenty-four years— the labour shortage hitherto is very much a shortage of very young workers—and so the differential between the teenage worker and the worker in his twenties gets narrower. And for those workers in their thirties, forties, and fifties, the differential has narrowed even more rapidly because there is no need to prevent them from leaving, as the young do if their wages are not increased. There is no shortage of elderly labour.

Thus a worker in his late fifties in a company like Company A may well earn little more, or even substantially less, than a worker of twenty-five years of age. In fact, Company A was currently employing five 'retired' workers from Isuzu Motors alone. These men had left Isuzu at the compulsory retiring age of fifty-five and had joined Company A at a monthly pay (¥22,000) which was less than half their income (c. ¥50,000) as regular employees of the big company. This is a very common pattern in Japan. In response to a suggestion that the experience of these far from senile workers might well compensate for a possibly lower level of energy, and that productivity differences might in fact be negligible, it was pointed out that in the big assembly plant such workers would usually have been very specialised. In the smaller company he would have to perform several operations, and his previous experience could well be irrelevant to some, if not all, of these processes. Furthermore, in this as in many other industries, technological change has been so rapid that the older workers' knowledge of certain machines and techniques could soon become obsolete, and generally speaking he would be less adaptable and dexterous than the school leaver. The decline in the once very high proportion of second-hand assets in the smaller firms lessens the value of the older, experienced worker from the 'parent' company, but in many small firms he must still be transferring to familiar equipment, since it is unlikely that technological change has been so rapid as to render him completely out of date. Company A, as a favoured medium-scale company, was no doubt typical of the more progressive, more technically up-to-date business, the emergence of which is necessary if industrial structure is to be improved, but one must not exaggerate the change.

For Company A the assembler has been, as we have seen, a financial guarantor, a source of technical assistance, a source of new and second-hand machinery, and even a source of labour. Yet Isuzu does not own this subcontractor, nor does it own any of its stock—although in Japanese industry stock-owning is not the powerful lever it can be in Britain, for example. Neither is it the sole customer for Company A, which did work for nine other companies, plus work for a subsidiary of Isuzu. In all, work for 11 companies involved a great variety of products, and this is often typical of the smaller concern. These products included, for the automobile industry, fan pulleys, inlet and exhaust manifolds, tie-rods and brackets; for the Honda Company, cylinder blocks for 120 c.c. motor-cycles; for the Niigata Ironworks (specialists in machinery for shipbuilding) friction clutches; and various parts for machine tools and construction machinery, for machines used in the processed food industry, and for railway machinery.

But this diversity was combined with a great dependence on Isuzu

TABLE 26: *Sales Structure of Company A:*
Sales Proceeds for the Six Months from
May to October, 1963

Customer	Sales (May–October) ¥	% of Total Sales
Isuzu Motors . .	141,355,046	73·1
Taikin Manufacturing .	10,536,482	5·4
Sub-Total . .	151,891,528	78·5
Niigata Ironworks .	28,071,050	14·5
Komatsu Manufacturing	3,101,206	1·6
Hino Motors . .	3,116,774	1·6
Others (6 companies) .	7,194,266	3·7
Total . . .	193,374,824	100·0

Motors and its subsidiary, Taikin Manufacturing, as the above sales analysis shows, and until very recently the dependence was even greater than in 1963, for it was only in 1961 that Company A began making friction clutches for the Niigata Ironworks, which was absorbing $14\frac{1}{2}\%$ of the sales in 1963. The diversification had slightly weakened the correlation between fluctuations in the automobile industry and the fortunes of Company A, but only very slightly, because $78\frac{1}{2}\%$ of total sales were still going to Isuzu and Taikin Manufacturing.

III

Company A is a good example of the medium-scale companies which are included in the small-medium enterprise problem. For the reasons given above it has a promising future, and in the Conclusion to this essay we shall consider some other factors which afford considerable hope that so far as this type of company is concerned the problem of dualism will not be quite so intractable as it seems today. But there are other groups of businesses which present a different picture. If A's dependence on Isuzu was high, the dependence of yet smaller firms on A, which itself subcontracted various processes, was often overwhelming, and in some instances amounted to 100%. Sometimes this was ultimately a 100% dependency on Isuzu or Honda via A, or via A and one or more other intermediaries. To find the ultimate destination of a part processed in a tiny two-man workshop, one may have to trace links between three, four or more companies. Occasionally one finds that the relationship is no different from that between the cottage-workers and the merchant-capitalist in the putting-out system in nineteenth and pre-nineteenth century European industry.

In fact, Company A and its business connections illustrate not only problems of capital supply, technological development, and the varied aspects of the structure of industrial employment in Japan since before the Second World War (as in, for instance, the career of A's founder), but also the extremely complex organisation of Japanese industry. We shall now turn to three small businesses which were lower down the scale from A, and which appear to be quite typical of the different grades of small enterprise in Japan.[11]

First, Company B, which consisted of the master, two office girls, and sixteen shopfloor workers. Until 1950 the master was a foreman in a company of fifty workers which was subcontracting for a Tokyo electric meter company. The subcontractor went bankrupt in 1950, and B was without regular employment until 1953, when he set up a workshop with a capital of ¥50,000 (which was borrowed from his wife) and with a labour force of four young workers, to do work for Company A.[12] For some years he sold his entire product to A, but since 1961 he had switched to subcontracting for electrical equipment manufacturers, two of which were taking 90% of his sales in March, 1964. His dependence on A had fallen to 5%, but the latter had loaned him money for the purchase of machinery, so relationships were still close.

B owned all his machines. Apparently this had been made possible not so much by accumulating profits as by borrowing heavily from the Jōnan Credit Association.[13] His capital structure displayed in microcosm the problems which cause concern in Japan: heavy imdebtedness to banks, high interest burdens and very high loan: equity ratios. In this case the ratio was said to be 94:6.[14] which would be unbelievable but for the evident anxiety displayed over the current (spring 1964) tight money policy.[15] No further credit would be available from banks, and one of his customers, who took 70% of his sales and was a very big concern, had just cut his cash receipts from the usual proportion of 30% to 10%, the remaining 90% payable in bills. It was agreed that there was no way by which this kind of pressure could be answered.

Between January and March 1964, concern was expressed over the growing number of bankruptcies, which also included larger firms than usual. The bankruptcy statistics showed sharp increases over the corresponding months of 1963, and the chain reaction which the newspapers and government spokesmen were then constantly emphasising was affecting B. In a credit squeeze reserve deposits are increased, banks, which are chronically over-loaned, must restrict credit and call in money, big firms either feel the squeeze or use this as an excuse to impose adverse conditions and in their turn squeeze their subcontractors by paying a higher percentage in bills, and the pressure is thus passed down the scale to ever-smaller and weaker enterprises which cannot bear it. This small company[16] of eighteen employees, itself a subcontractor, had no less than five sub-sub-contractors—each of four or five workers—dependent on it for about 50% of their sales, and since B now proposed to make them accept payment, not in cash as hitherto, but two months after delivery, one of the reasons for the mounting bankruptcy statistics was clear.

There was very little scope for B himself to get extended payment terms for his production materials: his wholesalers were small and his method of payment was already in three month bills. The government's repeated statements that efforts must be made to provide greater credit facilities for small and medium-sized businesses, and the instructions issued in February 1964 that in the current credit squeeze special attention should be paid to the needs of small firms, were summarily dismissed by B as political gambits: print and practice were two different things and, in any case, no one believed that the eighteen-man concern was ever in anybody's mind—except as a political sop—when these statements were made. They applied only to the upper ranges of the small-medium group, to the companies with between 150 and 300 employees.

Next on the scale comes Enterprise C, where there was a total labour force of six, including the master and his brother. The master was absent, there appeared to be no office, and no one was prepared to stop work and talk. The small workshop was congested, dirty, extremely noisy, and even dangerous, since small, sharp pieces of metal shavings occasionally hurtled through the air. The pressure of work seemed intense. For these reasons this was, so far as information was concerned, the least satisfactory visit, but this workshop was said to be very representative of this scale of enterprise—there are many thousands of manufacturing workshops employing fewer than nine workers in Japan[17]—and it was a sharp reminder of the reality behind the talk of the 'evils of dualism' in Japan.

The workshop was concerned solely with operations on Honda 120 c.c. cylinder blocks, performed for Company A, so here we have an example of complete dependency. After leaving A these blocks passed through at least one more intermediate company (Nittō Metals) before reaching Honda, all of which illustrates the complex industrial structure, embracing tiny workshops, surrounding the world's greatest manufacturer of motor-cycles.

Since this small enterprise was 100% dependent upon A for its contracts, and since A owned all the machinery, it was natural to ask why the work was subcontracted, and not performed directly by A. The answer, which also applied to the existence of our final example, was that the work was too intensive and dirty to fit into the operations upon which A was now concentrating. Company A's workshops were destined to move still nearer to more streamlined, mass-production methods, which were a more profitable absorber of space and managerial ability, and the contrast with the general working conditions of those employed in A's plant would be too great.

D, our final example of small and medium-scale enterprise, was a two-man business (master and one employee) operating in a workshop which was just big enough to accommodate two men and a machine, and which was indistinguishable from the mixture of residential housing and tiny workshops surrounding it. Once again, this workshop's operations were 100% subcontracted from Company A, and consisted simply of drilling one type of automobile part which was supplied from Isuzu via Company A. The processing of some 4,000 of these units every month involved repetitive operations of extreme monotony, although the Heath-Robinson network of driving belts, contrived by the master to provide a degree of automatic operation to the machine, which had been supplied by A, no doubt caused some excitement at times.

Although this minute workshop was every bit as crowded, noisy and dirty as C's workshop, and the work was obviously carried on under all the pressures of a piece-rate system and the possibilities of mechanical failure, the master was willing to shut down his machine and talk for a while. Before setting up on his own—if one may speak of this enterprise as being in any real sense independent—in 1960, he had worked for eight years for a company of some 150 workers engaged in manufacturing pipe-cutting machinery. With a retirement allowance of some ¥280,000, reinforced by ¥200,000 borrowed from his sister-in-law, he and his wife (whose previous employment by an Isuzu subcontractor had provided the contact with Company

A) began subcontracting for A. His wife was replaced after about 18 months by his present employee.

The monthly receipts from A varied from ¥130,000 to ¥150,000. Since his employee's wages were ¥35,000 per month, and his running expenses were some ¥30,000 per month, the income to cover his own salary and profit, the interest on and repayments of his sister-in-law's loan, and a depreciation allowance for his equipment, was no more than ¥65,000 to ¥85,000 a month. He and his helper worked on average a nine hour day, excluding breaks and stoppages, six days a week.

These small and medium-scale enterprises illustrate the growth, the structure, and the problems of Japanese manufacturing industry. It may be that in the past the smaller types of enterprise performed useful functions in the Japanese economy, but it is difficult to believe that they can continue to be, in any sense, an efficient method of employing scarce labour resources. Thousands of them must disappear, but the history of Company A throws light on the direction in which, it is hoped in Japan, manufacturing industry will travel, and the plans for rationalisation and expansion which Company A and others like it have in hand are referred to in the following Conclusion to this essay.

REFERENCES

1 Tsūshōsangyōshō Jūkōgyō-kyoku Jidōsha-ka (Automobile Department of the Heavy Industry Bureau, Ministry of International Trade and Industry) (ed.), *Nihon no jidōsha kōgyō 1963–64* (The Japanese Automobile Industry, 1963–4), Tokyo, 1964, p. 39. According to fiscal 1962–63 statistics.

2 *Ibid.*, p. 258. Placings refer to the position at the end of 1962, and do not include three-wheeled vehicles, which proliferate on Japan's narrow and tortuous streets.

3 Of the top ten automobile producers, Brazil's production increased by 533% between 1957 and 1962 and Japan's by 445%. The remaining eight countries were Sweden (258%), Australia (217%), Italy (170%), West Germany (100%), France (66%), Britain (44%), Canada (24%), and the United States (14%).

4 Information about Company A and its activities was obtained from direct interview, and from its 1963 *Kaisha gaiyō* (Company Prospectus).

5 This automobile department was the origin of the Isuzu Motor Company.

6 In 1939 the Yen was worth 1*s*. 2*d*.

7 In value terms. In physical terms, Shinohara suggests, the proportion might be as high as 80%.

8 Miyohei Shinohara, *Growth and Cycles in the Japanese Economy*, pp. 24–25.

9 Cf. S. A. Broadbridge, 'Technological Progress and State Support in the Japanese Shipbuilding Industry', *Journal of Development Studies*, Vol. 1, No. 2, January, 1965, pp. 167–170.

10 Company A obviously shared in the trend towards concentration of High School graduates in firms of over 100 workers in the years after 1958. Firms of 100–499 employees obtained 40% of new high school graduates in 1962 compared with 36% in 1960, while small firms of up to 99 employees secured only 21%, compared with 37%. These figures, which refer to manufacturing industry only, are from Rōdōshō Rōdō-tōkei Chōsa-bu (Department of Labour Statistics and Research, Ministry of Labour), *Rōdō hakusho 1963 nenkan* (White Paper on Labour for 1963), Tokyo, 1963, p. 91.

11 What follows was made possible by the kindness of the general manager of Company A, who took me to these workshops.

12 In 1953 Company A had a workforce of about fifty, yet this small company was in fact even then controlling a considerably larger volume of production than that yielded by its own shops, by letting out work to very small subcontractors.

13 Mentioned above, p. 75, as one of A's sources of credit.

14 Paid-up capital was ¥500,000; borrowed capital was ¥8 million.

15 See above, pp. 66–70.

16 Limited liability had been adopted in 1958, as investment increased and the payroll grew.

17 To be more precise, 344,000 in 1961. See above, Table 15, p. 55.

Conclusion

The bankruptcies described in Chapter 3 continued at a high level throughout 1964 and into 1965, and the credit squeeze was not relaxed until the anniversary of its inauguration in December 1963: by December 1964 the balance of payments deficit had been cured, at least temporarily. Increasingly, during the summer of 1964, medium-large companies joined small-medium businesses in a comradeship of financial difficulties, and, increasingly, big concerns failed to provide the help expected by both their proteges and by the financial press. Once again there was ample scope for pessimistic analysis of the many defects of the Japanese economy: to the evils of dualism and the always uncertain state of Japan's trade and exchange position was added a resuscitation of critical comment on the methods the Japanese employ in financing their industrial expansion. It is worth quoting the London *Economist* on this:[1]

> For years foreign businessmen in Japan have gritted their teeth every time some visitor has spouted the usual admiration for Japan's supposed industrial miracle and quietly swallowed their own deeply felt reservations. Japan's amazing industrial growth, they say, is no miracle. It is merely the result of ignoring all the conventional safeguards and tried practices of business financing. The Japanese have been able to get away with it for a long time, but at last the tiny cracks are widening into cracks wide enough to tumble the medium-size companies established in the shadows of their also under-capitalised mammoth cousins.

This kind of criticism has been voiced time and time again during the past century of Japan's economic growth, usually with the idea in the background that one possible path to growth is a combination of periods of spectacular investment and boom with periods of retrenchment, elimination of the inefficient by bankruptcy, and of consolidation.[2] The article in *The Economist* went on to suggest that Japan was in

> yet another stage in the well tried process of the big battalions of Japanese industry gobbling up the small fry.

As in Germany, industrial growth in Japan has been much more

closely based on banking finance than in Britain. We have seen how
the *zaibatsu* grew in power, coming to dominate not only large
sectors of the industrial world, but also great chunks of finance and
commerce. We have also illustrated the commonly known fact that
equity-loan ratios in the capital structures of industrial companies
are very low compared with Britain, ratios which are said to be much
lower than before the Second World War. In 1935, 68% of industrial
funds raised, apart from reserves and depreciation, were derived
from sales of stock; in 1963, the figure had fallen to 10%. Loans
from banks and other private financial institutions had risen from
30% to 80% of total industrial funds in the same period.[3] But the
major banks retain many of the old *zaibatsu* connections and
characteristics, and it is doubtful whether the financing of industrial
development is really so unsound as it is made to appear. With a
government commitment to growth such as Japan possesses one can
no more envisage the possibility of a banking crisis being allowed to
cripple industrial development than one can seriously contemplate
the possibility of governments in France, Britain or the United
States employing the methods of 1929–1933 to combat a depression.

What is relevant, however, is the lever afforded to the government
in controlling industrial growth by this system of industrial financing.
Perhaps the crucial point is not that raised by the debate on the
soundness or otherwise of Japan's variance from 'tried practices
of business financing', but the sharp impact of any deliberate attempt
to check growth. This is what makes the years 1963 to 1965 so
interesting in the context of government policy towards the dual
industrial structure, especially as the squeeze of these years followed
so hard on the heels of the previous check in 1961 to 1962. This had
been caused by a similarly vast deficit on current account with the
outside world, incurred during the latter stages of the great boom
of 1959 to 1961, and fits into a picture of consolidation and retrenchment from 1961 to 1965. Professor Allen has provided earlier
examples of conscious deflation being pursued after rapid expansion.[4]

In October 1963 the incumbent Director-General of the Japanese
Government's Economic Planning Agency announced that it was
time to enter 'Round 2' of the National Income Doubling Plan.[5]
This Plan was born in 1959 during a period of exceptionally fast
economic growth, when it had become clear that the existing Long-
Range Economic Plan[6] hopelessly understated the growth potential
of the Japanese economy: many of the targets set for 1962 were
already being achieved. The new Plan was approved in December
1960, and published in 1961 as the *New Long-Range Economic
Plan of Japan* (*1961–1970*) and sub-titled *Doubling National Income*

Plan.[7] The principal target of the Plan was to raise the gross national product from the ¥13 million million of 1960 to ¥26 million million in 1970.[8]

Economic growth in Japan since 1959 has more than fulfilled the annual advances required by this target. As we have seen, an outstanding characteristic of this growth has been the emphasis placed on heavy industry, on shipbuilding and other heavy engineering, including commercial vehicles and railway rolling stock, on steel and chemical plant, with a heavy investment in oil-refining. And we have also considered the relationship this growth has borne to the problem of dualism in the industrial structure. Critics have insisted that government policies, far from alleviating the problem, as promised by officials, have increased the gaps between different sections of the community. They point to the much faster rate of growth in productivity in industry compared with agriculture which, they say, has worsened economic dualism, and to the more rapid growth in productivity in the big companies than in those plants with fewer than 1000 workers which, they say, has worsened industrial dualism. True, wage differentials in manufacturing have narrowed somewhat, but the absolute shortfall in the wages of the workers in the smaller enterprises has considerably increased: in 1955 the average annual wage in medium-scale plants (100–299) was ¥165,000–¥105,000 less than the average wage in plants of 1000 or more workers. By 1961 this shortfall had increased to ¥142,000.[9] The trouble is, of course, that the penalty for being in a smaller firm was so huge in 1955 that there would have had to be an enormous relative deterioration in the status of the big companies' workforce materially to have reduced the absolute gap in incomes.

Heavy industry and large-scale enterprise are not necessarily cognate terms, but government emphasis on the development of heavy industry, allied as it is to the widespread belief that it is necessary to be big to survive in the world of international competition, has encouraged the growth of the giant concern. Investment funds have been channeled into those sectors where technological necessities have predicated large-scale developments: shipbuilding and heavy engineering are good examples. Concern with export markets has had a similar effect, and even the expansion of lighter engineering, particularly electrical equipment, has been accompanied by the establishment of huge, modern assembly plants.

The importance of any policy decisions affecting Japan's foreign trade can hardly be overemphasised. As the current economic plan says:[10]

. . . the balance of payments constituted the major ceiling on the post-war economic growth of the Japanese economy . . . exports hold the key to the success of the entire program.

The major trends in the composition of Japan's exports since the early 1950s have been a considerable shift from the traditional dependence on light industrial goods, particularly on textiles, and as Table 27 shows, an increasing emphasis on machinery of all kinds. The Income Doubling Plan proposed to increase the proportion of heavy machinery to 37 % by 1970, and of all machinery to 41·3 %, which are tremendous increases over the figures for the mid-1950s. Textiles, which reached 40 % of all exports in 1954, would decline steadily in importance until they constituted no more than $18\frac{1}{2}$ % of trade receipts. They were already down to a quarter in 1962. With deficits on current account reaching $1000 million in 1961 and $800 million in 1963, success in developing the industries producing machinery and metals is vitally important, and policies will inevitably continue to emphasise the growth of large-scale industry.

It is this juxtaposition of positive encouragement of the large-scale sector, and of constant reiteration of the need to help small and medium-sized businesses, that has led to widespread cynicism about government policy statements. In October 1963, Kenichi Miyazawa the former Director-General of the Economic Planning Agency, voiced one of the justifications for the emphasis on heavy industry in his announcement of 'Round 2' of the Income Doubling Plan. 'Round 1', he said, was designed to achieve international levels of industrialisation in the large-scale sector. This had been successful, but great problems of industrial structure remained. It was time, therefore, to enter 'Round 2' of the Plan, a phase which would solve both the agricultural problem, and the problem of small and medium-scale enterprise. To this end, there would be increases in budgetary provision for smaller businesses, the city banks were urged to switch their emphasis to loans for modernising the smaller firms, and the traditional financial organs of small-scale enterprise—the credit associations and the mutual loan and savings banks—were to expand their activities in cooperation with the various public banks associated with financing small business.[11]

These statements were dismissed in some quarters as mere pre-election gambits: polling in the general election was due on 21 November 1963. All parties were quick to express concern for the underprivileged sectors of Japanese society, and analysts were busy blaming dualism for the current price inflation: the flow of funds to

Commodities	1952	1953	1954	1955	1956	1957	1958	1959	1960	1961	1962	1970
Machinery and transport equipment	9	9	12	12	19	22	22	23	23	26	25	37·0
Metals and metal products	27	15	15	19	14	11	13	12	14	13	15	11·2
Chemicals	3	5	5	5	5	5	5	5	4	5	5	5·3
Sub-totals	*39*	*29*	*32*	*36*	*38*	*38*	*40*	*40*	*41*	*44*	*45*	*53·5*
Textiles	36	36	40	37	35	35	31	30	30	27	25	18·5
Food and Drink	8	10	8	7	7	6	8	7	6	6	7	5·9
Others	17	25	20	20	20	21	21	23	23	23	23	22·1
Sub-totals	*61*	*71*	*68*	*64*	*62*	*62*	*60*	*60*	*59*	*56*	*55*	*46·5*
Grand Totals	100	100	100	100	100	100	100	100	100	100	100	100·0

Note: percentages for 1952-1962 are calculated from figures given in the following sources:

1952–55: Nihon Kaihatsu Ginkō Chōsa-bu (Research Division of the Japan Development Bank), *Tōkei yōran 1958* (Statistical Survey for 1958), Tokyo, 1958, p. 20.

1956–61: Ditto, *Tōkei yōran 1962* (Statistical Survey for 1962), Tokyo, 1962, p. 27.

1962: Tsūshōsangyō Daijin Kambō Chōsa-tōkei-bu (Research and Statistical Section of the Secretariat of the Minister for International Trade and Industry), *Tsūshōsangyō tōkei yōran Shōwa 38 nen* (Statistical Survey of Trade and Industry for 1963), Tokyo, 1963, pp. 56–57.

1970: *Doubling Plan*, p. 77.

large-scale enterprise starved small and medium-sized businesses (and also agriculture) of investment funds; this resulted in the low productivity of these sectors, which, with wages and other costs steadily rising, was responsible for the sharp inflation in the prices of consumer goods. The consumer price index had been rising some 7% per annum for the past three years, reflecting what the Income Doubling Plan termed 'vigorous investments in industrial facilities'.[12] At the time it was possible to argue that since 1965 was to be the year of the 'open economy'—of important moves towards trade and exchange liberalisation—the promise of help for small businesses reflected a genuine desire to improve industrial efficiency as part of a wider effort to extricate Japan from its poor international payments position. Even then, however, the problem which bothered many was the apparent impossibility of reconciling promises which blanketed the whole of the small-scale sector, with the obvious financial necessity of helping only those that were worth helping.

It now seems likely that the years 1963 to 1965, and possibly the whole period from 1961 to 1965 will join other periods as an example of the weeding-out process. The government, faced with a balance of payments crisis, and a soaring industrial production index, at the end of 1963, followed up its promises of help with a tight money policy which altered the business climate to such an extent that bankruptcies of smaller firms reached record figures. Instead of bolstering the little man, 'Round 2' saw hundreds of his kind counted out. The process by which 'rationalisation' was achieved was traced in Chapter 4, in the account of how the squeeze could be shifted to small firms. Unit prices for parts-manufacturers were cut, cash proportions of accounts were slashed, bill-periods extended, and so on.

The credit squeeze of 1964 provided a spur, if not an excuse, for 'parent' companies to shed the more inefficient of their sub-contractors. It is difficult to see how dual characteristics can be eliminated in any other way in a country like Japan. The government tried to soften the blow by compelling banks to stop the forced-deposit system, by easing inland-revenue payments, and by encouraging public corporations and public utilities to accept payment of accounts by instalments. These measures need not be dismissed as mere political soporifics, and there is no logical contradiction in a combination of a general credit squeeze and selective help: the really insolvent or redundant would and should go under the impact of the squeeze, while those who could survive with the help of these measures deserved to be helped. An added virtue of the process from the political point of view was the appearance of taking all possible steps to fulfill past pledges. Opposition parties were naturally quick to level accusations of bad faith at the government.

Probably more important in the long-run than any temporary palliative is the effect of the attitude of big companies towards their subcontractors and industrial customers. Where the big company shares the growing belief that small companies exist, not to be exploited, but to be re-organised and re-equipped to increase productivity on a broad front, substantial progress can be made. Indeed, given the present structure of the capital and money markets in Japan, this is probably the only path for industrial change to follow. The relationships of Company A to the great automobile assembler which bought the bulk of its products are a good illustration of what can be achieved, and are also a pointer to the future. This company of 150 workers was still small, but expansion since the mid-1950s had been substantial. Moreover, it had recently (in August, 1963) joined with five other subcontractors for Isuzu to float a new and separate company in which greater specialisation would be possible. The plan was to combine within one plant processes which were hitherto carried on in the six separate companies, processes which could be performed on a continuous flow basis, once the market was big enough. As the automobile industry grows, and as small companies combine under the auspices of the great assemblers, it will be possible for mass-production techniques to be adopted where at present each producer's capacity and market are so small that labour-intensive and discontinuous methods of operation are the only ones possible.[13]

It is therefore no longer always true that subcontracting relationships between big and medium-sized companies in Japan are primarily those of the exploiters and the exploited. Nor is it true, therefore, that the big assembler is only interested in maintaining large numbers of small subcontractors and suppliers whom he can exploit in the traditional ways. More emphasis now seems to be placed on the link between the efficiency of the subcontractors and parts-manufacturers, and the competitive power of their respective assemblers. The line-up of the future is between a few very powerful motor-companies—to continue with the example of the automobile industry—each of which will support the efforts of its numerous suppliers and contractors to cooperate, modernise, and expand. This explains the extensive assistance given in the form of technical advice, the sale and loan of machines, and the guaranteeing of loans.

There is a growing conviction in Japan that, quite apart from social considerations, it is vital to improve the operations of the smaller businesses, if both greater efficiency in production for the

H

domestic market and improved international competitive power is to be achieved. The successes gained so far in the export drive, and in the expansion and modernisation of heavy industry, may well be hitting a ceiling set by poor performance in the industries which feed glamorous exporters like shipbuilding and electrical goods, and by the drying up of the one-time abundant reservoir of agricultural labour. Since the big and the small company are woven together in an intricate pattern of industrial relationships it is of crucial importance, in the competitive conditions of the future, to maximise productivity on a broader front. With the slowing down in the rate of population growth, and the exhaustion of agricultural labour reserves, the inefficient background to the great modern steel firm, shipyard, synthetic yarn spinner, and automobile plant, will become more and more of a drag on the economy's performance.

It is true that there is always the possibility of a further reorganisation of agriculture, which might alter the picture considerably. Japan's industrial progress so far has been closely associated with the comparatively rapid run-down of its agricultural labour force from 38% of the national workforce in 1955 to 25% in 1962. But for one-quarter of the country's workers to be engaged in agriculture is a great contrast to many of the leading industrial nations of the world and indicates that there is still scope for a redistribution of resources. This large agricultural labour force produces only one-seventh of the national income and forms part of yet another serious problem. But there are many in Japan who believe that, great as the agricultural population still is, any future change will be very, very slow. Farm structures have, it is said, become solidified after Land Reform, and there is little chance of any further mass exodus from the land.

It is all the more important, therefore, that urban labour is fully and effectively utilised. The tertiary sector absorbs a huge number of people for a country with a per capita income which is very low by the standards of Western Europe, and for an economy which is said to be suffering from a labour shortage. Many thousands of entrepreneurs in both the tertiary and the manufacturing sectors are generally regarded as living on lower incomes than their employed counterparts, and we know that their employees in general receive much lower wages than those employed in bigger companies. There is obvious economic waste here, which impinges on distribution costs and retail prices, as well as on manufacturers' costs; furthermore, lack of social security, together with early retirement practices, contribute to the comparative ease with which smaller firms have been able to obtain labour, particularly in recession, and also to the pressure of would-be entrepreneurs in already crowded fields of activity. Japan, therefore, still faces serious structural problems, but some of these obstacles to improvement should weaken as both economic development and social welfare policies increase in strength. In many sectors of industry itself positive measures are being taken to modernise production right down the line to the smaller of the medium-sized plants.

As in other countries, there will always be scope for smaller firms. In those sectors which continue to cater for highly specialised and traditional consumption needs, the small firm may well be the most economic unit, and it need not possess the characteristics which are condemned as dualistic. But for the many thousands of very small units in manufacturing industries which supply the mass-produced articles common to all advanced industrial nations, the future must be bleak. It is not merely that wage and productivity levels are so much lower in these firms, but quite simply that far too many people work in very small plants—if western industrial nations are a valid guide. For these the solution must be elimination, although since one-third of the workers in small and medium businesses of all sectors are self-employed or family workers, this will be a slow and very probably a painful process. The bad features of this part of dualism may even be accentuated through the ability of the family workers in such units to accept reductions in a per capita income. But this is likely to happen more in distribution and services than in the general range of manufacturing, where very small businesses should disappear much more quickly. It is at least possible that the upward shift in scale, with more effective and expanding medium-sized firms emerging from the reorganisation of the big companies' suppliers, will be faster in the 1960s than it was in the 1950s. The middle group of firms, the weakness of which has been one of the major features of Japanese industrial structure, may then be able to narrow the productivity gap which, as we have seen, was not only depressingly large in 1961, but had actually been increasing since 1955. It is, indeed, possible that 1961 marked a turning point: some productivity differentials began to narrow in 1961–1963, while others at least ceased to widen.[14] This trend, which no doubt reflects the changing relationships between large and medium companies, may well be one of the 'signs that the duality in the economy [is] approaching its term.'[15]

REFERENCES

1 *The Economist*, 13 March, 1965.

2 Cf. G. C. Allen, 'Factors in Japan's Economic Growth', in C. D. Cowan (ed.), *op. cit.*, pp. 196–204.

3 Japan Development Bank, *Facts and Figures on the Japanese Economy*, Tokyo, 1964, p. 150.

4 In 'Factors in Japan's Economic Growth', *op. cit.* These were the deflations of the early 1880's and of 1927–1931.

5 *Nihon Keizai Shimbun*, 12 October, 1963.

6 Economic Planning Agency, Japanese Government, *New Long-Range Economic Plan of Japan* (*FY 1958–FY 1962*), Tokyo, n.d.

7 Economic Planning Agency, Japanese Government, Tokyo, 1961. Hereafter cited as *Doubling Plan*.

8 *Doubling Plan*, p. iii. Figures are in fiscal 1958 prices.

9 See above, Table 22, p. 64.

10 *Doubling Plan*, p. 74.

11 *Nihon Keizai Shimbun*, 18 November, 1963.

12 *Doubling Plan*, p. 23.

13 The Japanese term for this evolving system of production–relationships is *kigyō keiretsu*, which could be translated as 'an integrated series of companies'. G. C. Allen's latest book, *Japan's Economic Expansion*, London, 1965, contains a discussion of *keiretsu* which suggests that the system 'has had the effect of circumscribing co-operative activities among small and medium manufacturers.' (p. 115) It should be made clear that Allen is referring to formal co-operative associations, whereas the co-operation I have mentioned is independent of these co-operatives, and is sometimes the only alternative to elimination from the *keiretsu* as the large company enforces an increase in scale and in specialization.

14 Cf. Smaller Enterprise White Paper, *op. cit.*, p. 323.

15 Cf. G. C. Allen, *Japan's Economic Expansion*, *op. cit.*, p. 114.

Bibliography

This bibliography contains only those works cited in the text which refer specifically to Japan. Further reading may be obtained from Miyohei Shinohara's *Survey of Japanese Literature on the Small Industry*, which is mentioned in the preface to this essay.

A. *Works in Japanese*

Akashi, Teruō and Suzuki, Norihisa, *Nihon kinyū-shi* (A History of Japanese Finance), Vol. 1, Tokyo, 1957.

Asahi Shimbun-sha (Asahi News Ltd.) *Asahi Shimbun*, 1963–64.

Chūshō Kigyō-chō (Smaller Enterprise Agency), *Chūshō kigyō hakusho Shōwa 38 nendo* (White Paper on Small-Medium Enterprise), Tokyo, 1964; *Chūshō kigyō kindaika no jitsumu* (The Administration of the Modernisation of Small-Medium Enterprise), Tokyo, 1964.

Echigo, Kazunori, *Nihon zōsen kōgyō-ron* (An Essay on the Japanese Shipbuilding Industry), Tokyo, 1956.

Fukushima, Masao, 'Meiji shonen no keizai seisaku to shihon chikuseki no mondai' (Economic Policy in the Early Meiji Period and the Problem of Capital Accumulation), *Tōyō Bunka*, No. 9, 1952.

Ikeuchi, Nobuyuki, *Kigyō shūchū-ron* (An Essay on Business Concentration), Tokyo, 1964.

Institute of Economic Research, Hitotsubashi University, *Annotated Economic Statistics of Japan for Postwar Years up to 1958*, Tokyo, 1961. (In Japanese).

Itō, Yuzuru, 'Kangin ruinen kashitsuke-daka no dōkō: keizai hatten to fudōsan ginkō' (Fluctuations in the Annual Advances of the Hypothec Bank: Economic Growth and the Mortgage Bank), *Nōgyō Keizai Kenkyū*, Vol. 24, No. 3, February, 1953.

Keizai Kikaku-chō (Economic Planning Agency), *Kokumin shotoku hakusho Shōwa 37 nendo* (National Income White Paper for 1962–63), Tokyo, 1964.

Keizai Shingikai (Economic Deliberation Council), *Kokumin shotoku baizō keikaku chūkan kentō hōkoku* (Report on the Interim Study of the National Income Doubling Plan), Tokyo, 1964.

Kotani, Chiaki, *Nihon no kōgyō shihon* (Industrial Capital in Japan), Tokyo, 1960.

Misonou, Hitoshi, 'Nihon dokusen shihon no kyōka to teichaku' (The Strengthening of Monopoly Capital in Japan), *Keizai Hyōron*, May, 1964.

Miyashita, Takehei, 'Zōsen kōgyō no hatten to kōzō' (The Development and Structure of the Shipbuilding Industry) *in* Arisawa, Hiromi (ed.),

Gendai Nihon sangyō kōza (Modern Japanese Industry), Vol. V: *Kikai kōgyō* (Machine Industries), Pt. 1, Tokyo, 1961.

Namiki, Nobuyoshi, 'Jūkōgyōka no genjō to shōrai' (The Present Situation and Future of Heavy-Industrialisation), *in* Shinohara, Miyohei (ed.), *Nihon keizai no jūkōgyōka* (The Heavy-Industrialisation of the Japanese Economy), Tokyo, 1964.

Nagasu, Kazuji, *Nihon keizai nyūmon* (An Introduction to the Japanese Economy), Tokyo, 1960.

Nihon Kaihatsu Ginkō Chōsabu (Research Division of the Japan Development Bank), *Chōsa geppō* (Monthly Bulletin), Vol. 12, Nos. 4–5, July, 1963 and Vol. 13, No. 1, April, 1964; *Tōkei yōran 1958* and *1962* (Statistical Survey for 1958, and for 1962), Tokyo, 1958 and 1962.

Nihon Keizai Shimbun-sha (Japan Economic News Ltd.), *Nihon Keizai Shimbun* (Japan Economic News), 1963–1964.

Ōkita, Saburo, *Nihon keizai no seichō to kōzō* (The Growth and Structure of the Japanese Economy), Tokyo, 1962.

Rōdōshō Rōdō Tōkei Chōsabu (Department of Labour Statistics and Research, Ministry of Labour), *Rōdō hakusho 1963 nenkan* (White Paper on Labour for 1963), Tokyo, 1963.

Shinohara, Miyohei (ed), *Sangyō kōzō* (The Structure of Industry), Tokyo, 1962.

Tatsumi, Nobuharu, *Dokusen dankai ni okeru chūshō kigyō no kenkyū* (Studies of Small-Medium Enterprise in the Monopoly Stage [of Capitalism]), Tokyo, 1960.

Tōbata, Seiichi and Ohkawa, Kazushi, *Nihon no keizai to nōgyō* (The Japanese Economy and Agriculture), Tokyo, 1962.

Tsuchiya, Takao, *Nihon no seishō* (Political Merchants of Japan), Tokyo, 1956; *Nihon keizai-shi* (An Economic History of Japan), Tokyo, 1963; *Zoku Nihon keizai-shi gaiyō* (An Outline Economic History of Japan, Vol. II), Tokyo, 1939.

Tsūshōsangyōshō Jūkōgyōkyoku Jidōsha-ka (Automobile Department of the Heavy Industry Bureau, Ministry of International Trade and Industry), *Nihon no jidōsha kōgyō 1963–4* (The Japanese Automobile Industry 1963–4), Tokyo, 1964.

Tsūshōsangyō Daijin Kambō Chōsa Tōkei-bu (Research and Statistical Section of the Secretariat of the Minister for International Trade and Industry), *Tsūshōsangyō tōkei yōran Shōwa 38 nen* (Statistical Survey of Trade and Industry for 1963), Tokyo, 1963.

Yamanaka, Tokutarō, *Keizai seichō to chūshō kigyō* (Economic Growth and the Smaller Enterprise), Tokyo, 1963.

B. *Works in English*

Allen, G. C. *A Short Economic History of Japan 1867–1937*, London, (2nd ed.), 1962; 'Factors in Japan's Economic Growth', *in* C. D. Cowan (ed.), *The Economic Development of China and Japan*, London, 1964; *Japan's Economic Expansion*, London, 1965.

Bisson, T. A. *Zaibatsu Dissolution in Japan*, Berkeley, 1954.

Broadbridge, S. A. 'Technological Progress and State Support in the Japanese Shipbuilding Industry', *Journal of Development Studies*, Vol. 1, No. 2, January, 1965.

Bureau of Statistics, Office of the Prime Minister, *Japan Statistical Yearbook 1962* and *1963*, Tokyo, 1963 and 1964.

Dore, R. P. *Education in Tokugawa Japan*, London, 1965.

Economic Counsel Board, Japanese Government, *Economic Survey of Japan (1953–1954)*, Tokyo, 1954.

Economic Planning Agency, Japanese Government, *Economic Survey of Japan (1961–1962)*, Tokyo, n.d. [1962]; *Economic Survey of Japan (1962–1963)*, Tokyo, n.d. [1963]; *New Long-Range Economic Plan of Japan (FY 1958–FY 1962)*, Tokyo, n.d. [1958?]; *New Long-Range Economic Plan of Japan (1961–1970)*, Tokyo, 1961.

Emi, Koichi, *Government Fiscal Activity and Economic Growth in Japan 1868–1960*, Tokyo, 1963.

Fujita, Masahiro, 'The Banking System in the Middle Meiji Era (1870–1910)', *Kobe Economic and Business Review*, No. 3, 1956.

Jansen, Marius B. *Sakamoto Ryōma and the Meiji Restoration*, Princeton, 1961.

Japan Development Bank, *Facts and Figures on the Japanese Economy*, Tokyo, 1964.

Japan Times Ltd., *Japan Times*, 1963–1964.

Lockwood, W. W. *The Economic Development of Japan: Growth and Structural Change 1868–1938*, Princeton, 1954; *The State and Economic Enterprise in Japan: Essays in the Political Economy of Growth*. Princeton, 1965.

Ministry of Labor, Division of Labor Statistics and Research, *Year Book of Labor Statistics 1962*, Tokyo, 1964.

Ohkawa, Kazushi and Rosovsky, Henry, 'Recent Japanese Growth in Historical Perspective', *American Economic Review*, Vol. LIII, No. 2, May, 1963.

Ranis, Gustav, 'Factor Proportions in Japanese Economic Development', *American Economic Review*, Vol. XLVII, No. 5, September, 1957.

Rosovsky, Henry, *Capital Formation in Japan 1868–1940*, Glencoe, Illinois, 1961.

Rosovsky, Henry and Ohkawa, Kazushi, 'The Indigenous Components in the Modern Japanese Economy', *Economic Development and Cultural Change*, Vol. IX, No. 3, April, 1961.

Schumpeter, E. B. (ed.), *The Industrialization of Japan and Manchukuo 1930–1940*, New York, 1940.

Shinohara, Miyohei, *Growth and Cycles in the Japanese Economy*, Tokyo, 1962; *Survey of Japanese Literature on the Small Industry, with Selected Bibliography*, privately printed, Hitotsubashi University, Tokyo, 1964.

Smith, T. C. *Political Change and Industrial Development in Japan: Government Enterprise 1868–1880*, Stanford, 1955.

Watanabe, T., 'Economic Aspects of Dualism in the Industrial Develop-
    ment of Japan', *Economic Development and Cultural Change*, Vol.
    XIII, No. 3, April, 1965.
Yamanaka, Tokutaro, *Small Business in Japan*, Tokyo, 1960.

INDEX

Accelerated depreciation, 76
Agriculture, 7, 9
  employment, 21–23, 27–30
  productivity, 21–22, 94
Aikawa, 37
Akashi, Teruō, 25n
Allen, G. C., 25n, 88, 96n
Arisawa, Hiromi, 24n
Asano, 37
Automobile industry, 34, 73, 74, 93

Balance of payments, 66, 87, 88, 90, 92
Banking system and industrial invest-
ment 12–16, 32–33, 54, 82, 87–88
Bank mergers, 16
Bank of England, 13
Bank of Japan, 14
  rate of discount, 66, 69
Bankruptcies, 47, 66–70, 83, 87, 92
Belgium, 16
Birmingham, 16
Bisson, T. A., 44n
Boulton & Watt, 16
Brazil, 73
Britain, 13, 17, 21, 28, 31, 32, 38, 40,
41, 42, 47, 48, 73, 78, 80, 88
  scale of manufacturing
  —and employment distribution, 50–
51
  —and wage differentials, 51–52
  —and productivity differentials, 52–
53
Broadbridge, S. A., 85n
Business taxation, 20

Capital
  accumulation, in England, 13, in
Japan, 14–15
  formation, 11, 19, 30–35
  intensity, 19–20, 28, 29, 30
  market, 12–16
  —output ratio, 63
Cement, 5, 31, 35
Central Co-operative Bank for Commerce and Industry, (Shōkō Kumiai
Chūō Kinko), 68

Central Government
  policies after Meiji Restoration,
10–12
  and banking system, 14–16
  and mobilization of capital, 14, 18–
21
  and industrial concentration, 16–18
  and consumption habits, 20
Chemical industry, 17, 34, 35, 39–40,
41
China, 8, 17, 30
Chūshō-kigyō (small-medium enter-
prise), 25n, 47
Credit associations (Shinyō Kinko), 75
Coal, 18, 32–35
Cole, W. A., 26n
Commercial classes, 8
Commercial vehicles, 5, 31, 40, 73
Consumption, personal, 4, 32–33, 40
Counterpart Fund, 32
Cowan, C. D., 25n

Daiichi, 38
Deane, Phyllis, 26n
Deflation, 88
Demant, V. A., 25n
Demonstration effect, 18–19
Dore, R. P., 25n

Echigo, Kazunori, 24n
Economic Counsel Board, 7n
Economic dualism
  in Italy, 5–6
  in Japan 3, 5, 7, 89
Economic Planning Agency (Keizai
Kikaku-chō), 7n, 44n, 88, 90
Economic plans, 7, 40, 42, 54, 88
Economic policy, 10–12, 32, 34, 40,
54, 66–70, 87–93
Economic structure
  effect of growth on, 7
  character of, 22, 42–43, 89
Economic Surveys of Japan, 3, 54
Electric power, 17, 32–35
Emi, Koichi, 25n